점프 업 파닉스 Jump Up Phonics 3 개정판

점프 업 파닉스 3 [개정판]

2008년 05월 20일 초판 1쇄 발행
2025년 04월 15일 개정 1쇄 발행

지은이 문호준/국제어학연구소 영어학부
그림 이경택
펴낸이 이규인
펴낸곳 국제어학연구소 출판부
출판등록 2010년 1월 18일 제302-2010-000006호
주소 서울특별시 마포구 대흥로4길 49, 1층(용강동 월명빌딩)
Tel (02) 704-0900 **팩시밀리** (02) 703-5117
홈페이지 www.bookcamp.co.kr
e-mail changbook1@hanmail.net
ISBN 979-11-9880104-3 13740
정가 18,000원

Jump Up Phonics 3

점프 업
파닉스

개정판

글 뮤호준·국제어학연구소 영어학부

ILR 국제어학연구소

CONTENTS

There is a naughty clam in the class.
The clam hides a black clock
from the jellyfish.
The clam hides a blue block
from the starfish.
The clam hides a red flag
from the octopus.
All the stuff is in the naughty clam.

Listen and repeat.

  _____

  _____

  _____

Match and write.

fl • • ack  •

bl • • am  •

cl • • ag  •

Listen, point and repeat.

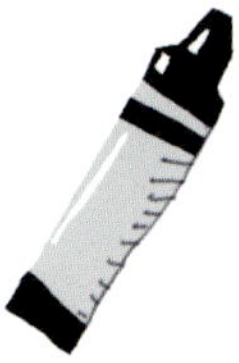

black	**bl**ue	**bl**ade
block	**cl**ass	**cl**ap
clock	**cl**am	**fl**at
flag	**fl**ame	**fl**ap

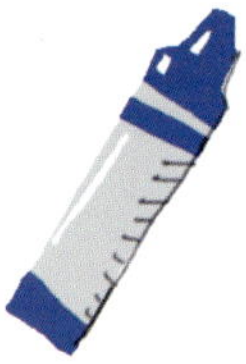

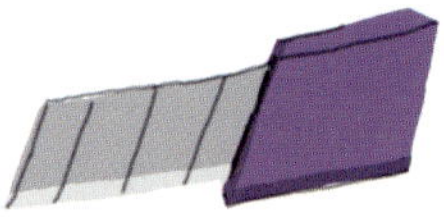

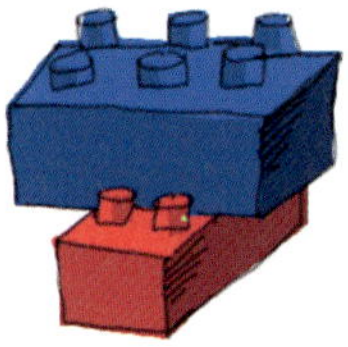

9

Circle the correct picture for the beginning sound.

1 **bl**

2 **cl**

3 **fl**

Listen, circle and write.

1

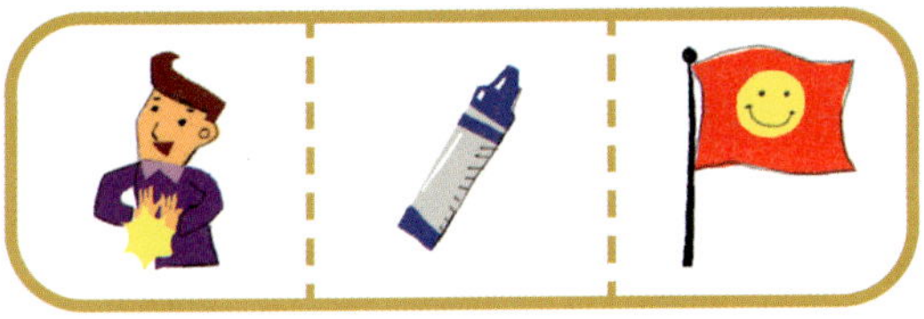

_____ ag

2

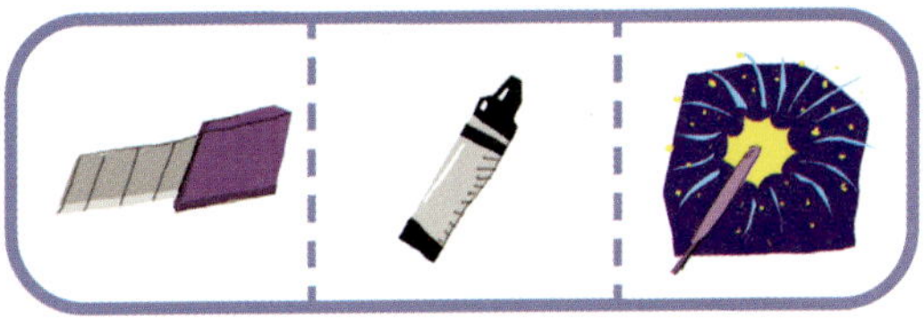

_____ ade

3

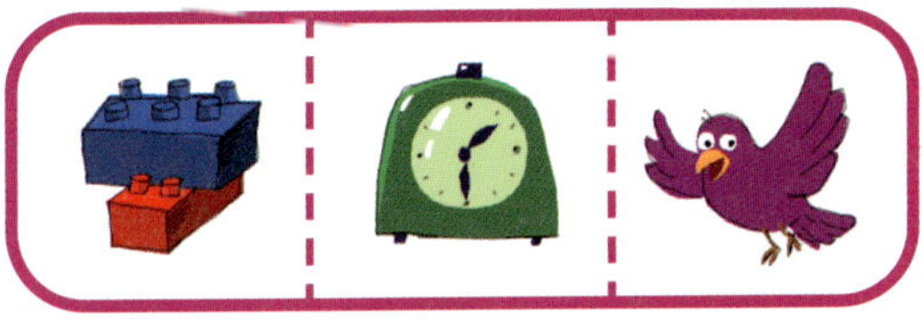

_____ ock

4

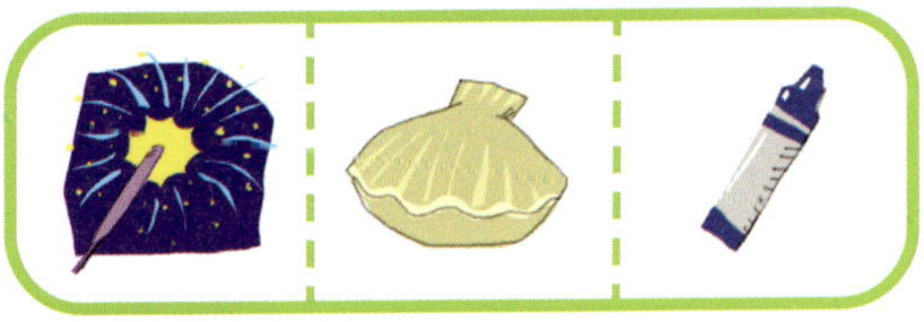

_____ am

5

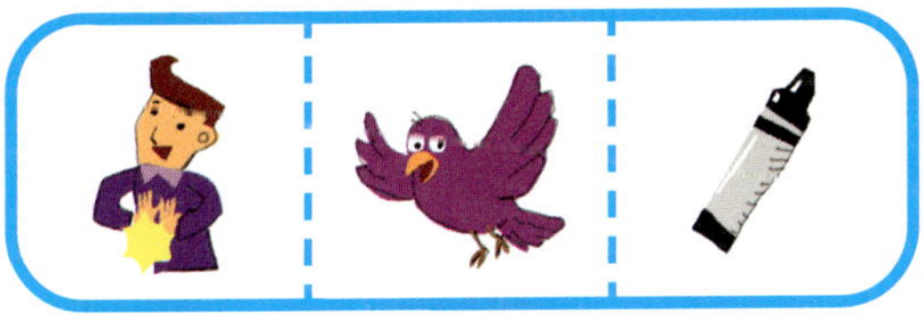

_____ ap

6

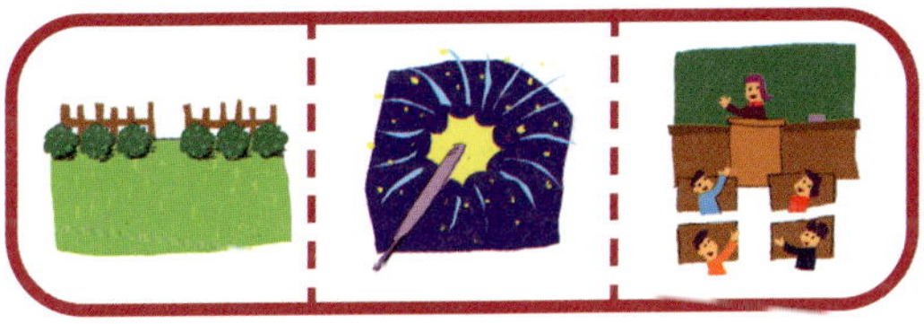

_____ ass

7

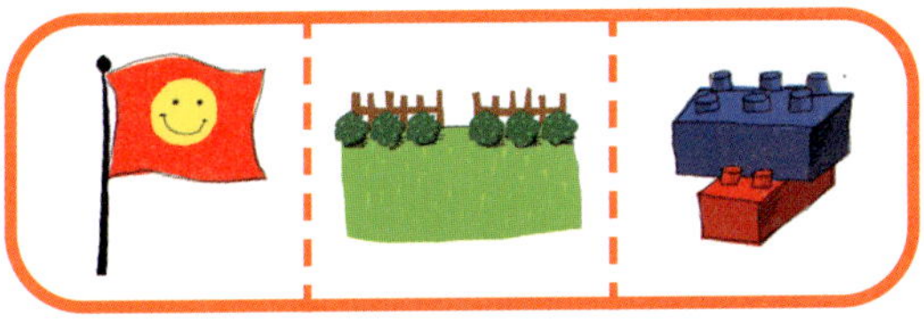

_____ at

8

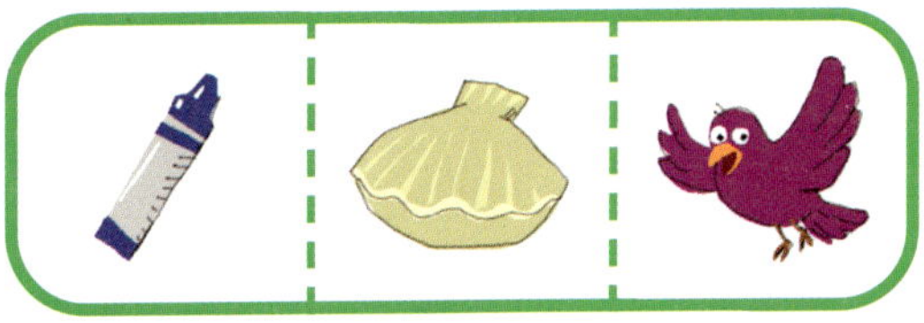

_____ ue

Read and find the correct sentence for the picture.

1

ⓐ The red flags flap in the wind. ✓

ⓑ The red hens clap their hands. ☐

2

ⓐ The kids pile the black blocks. ☐

ⓑ The kids pile the blue blocks. ☐

3

ⓐ The man uses a blade to cut the tape. ☐

ⓑ The man uses a block to cut the rope. ☐

4

ⓐ The clock is on the blue gate. ☐

ⓑ The flag is on the blue gate. ☐

5

ⓐ There is a fat pig in the class. ☐

ⓑ There is a cute clam in the class. ☐

6

ⓐ The men sit on the flat mat. ☐

ⓑ The men sit on the mat with flame. ☐

Color the beginning sound and write the word.

1
bl
cl
fl

clam

2
bl
cl
fl

3
bl
cl
fl

4
bl
cl
fl

5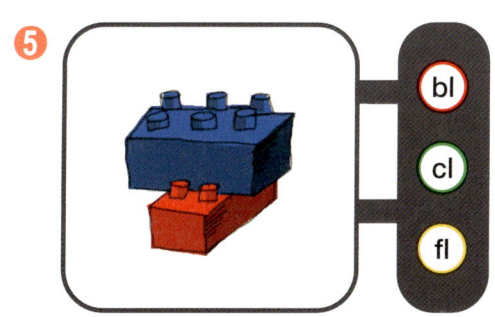
bl
cl
fl

6
bl
cl
fl

Word Search

Circle the words and complete the story.

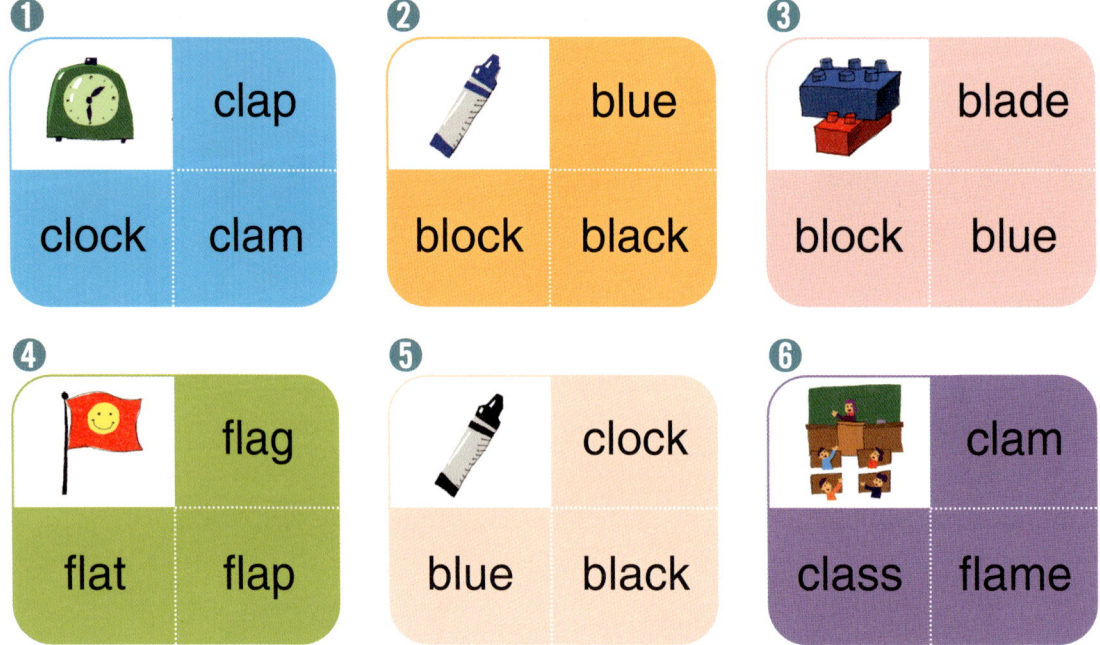

- There is a naughty clam in the _____ .

- The clam hides a _____ _____ from the jellyfish.

- The clam hides a _____ _____ from the starfish.

- The clam hides a red _____ from the octopus.

- All the stuff is in the naughty clam.

14

Activity *chant*

Black cat, black cat!
Are you ready?

Pick up the red flag.
Pick up the blue flag.

Black cat, black cat!
Are you ready?

Clap clap your hands.
Clap clap your hands.
One two three four five!

A crab weds a frog.

The crab is on the red brick.

The frog is on the blue block.

The crab bride is in a white dress.

They cut the cake with a blade.

The brass band plays music
in front of them.

Listen and repeat.

 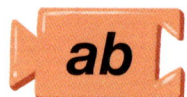 

Match and write.

cr  ab

fr  ick

br  og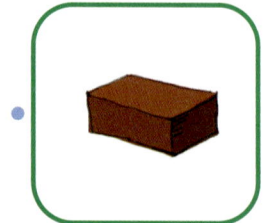

Listen, point and repeat.

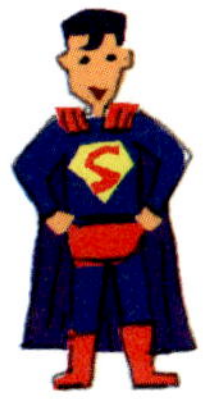

brave	**br**ick	**br**ide
brass	**cr**op	**cr**oss
crab	**cr**aft	**fr**og
frame	**fr**ont	**fr**om

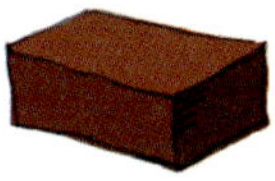

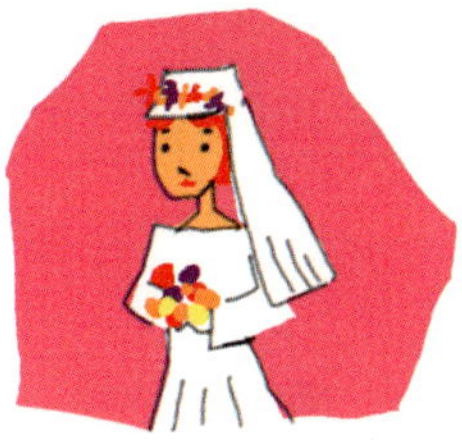

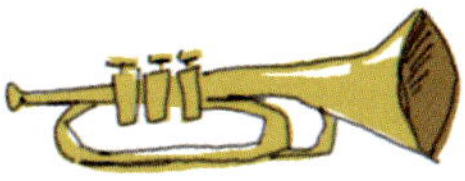

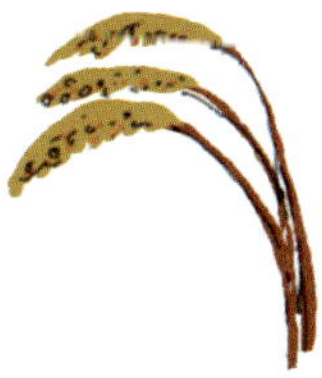

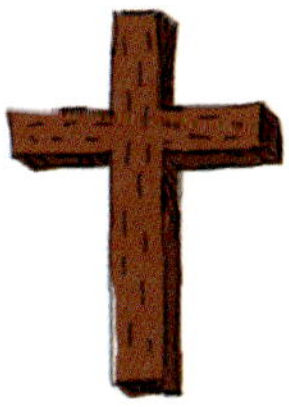

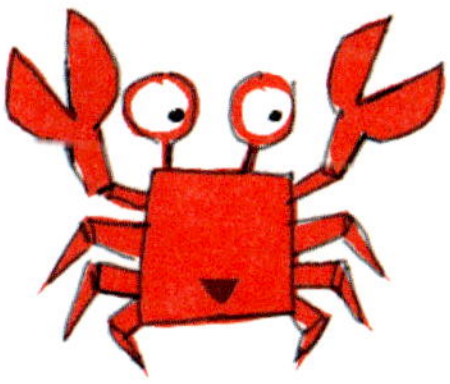

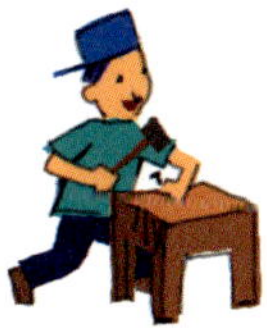

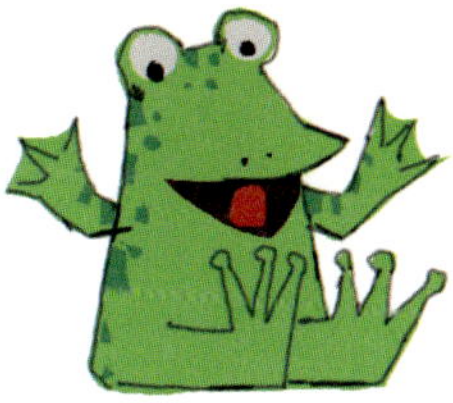

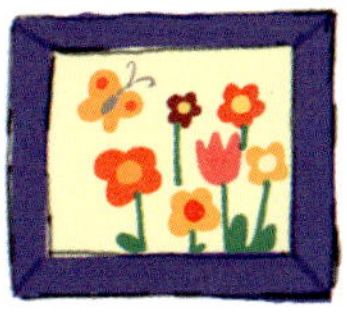

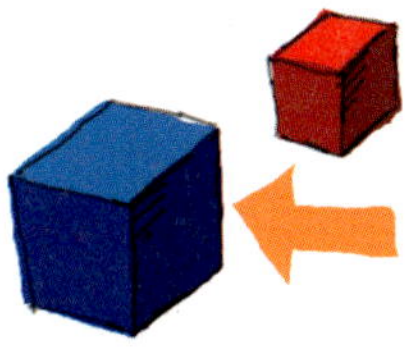

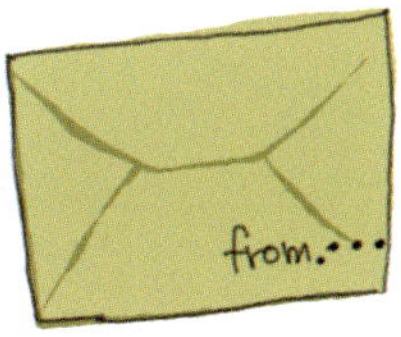

Circle the correct picture for the beginning sound.

1 **br**

2 **cr**

3 **fr**

Listen, circle and write.

1

_____ ave

2

_____ og

3

_____ ab

4

_____ ont

5

_____ ide

6
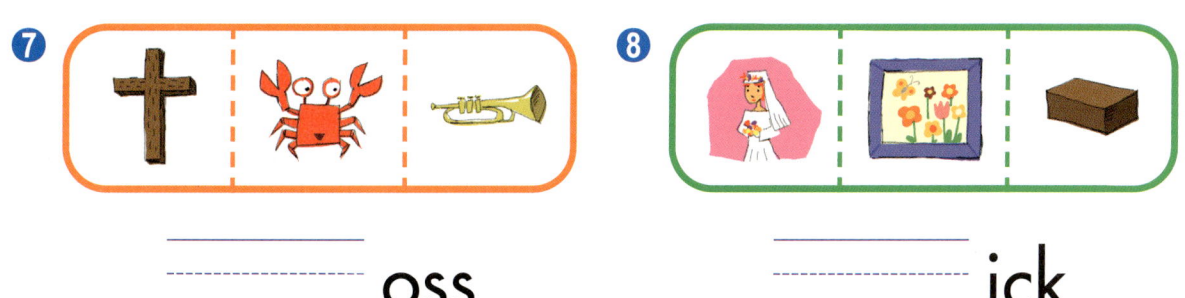

_____ op

7

_____ oss

8

_____ ick

21

Read and find the correct sentence for the picture.

ⓐ The brave bride hit the bad man. ☐

ⓑ The brave frog hit the bad man. ☐

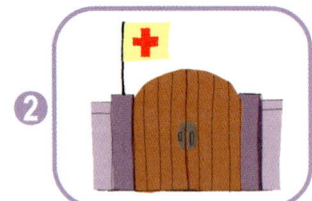

ⓐ The red cross flag is on the gate. ☐

ⓑ The red cross flag is in the frame. ☐

ⓐ The bride is in front of the gate. ☐

ⓑ The crab is in front of the hut. ☐

ⓐ The vase is on the brick. ☐

ⓑ The rose is on the bride. ☐

ⓐ Men wipe the brasses. ☐

ⓑ Men play the brasses. ☐

ⓐ The man has some crops. ☐

ⓑ The man has some crabs. ☐

Color the beginning sound and write the word.

1

br
cr
fr

2

br
cr
fr

3

br
cr
fr

4

br
cr
fr

5

br
cr
fr

6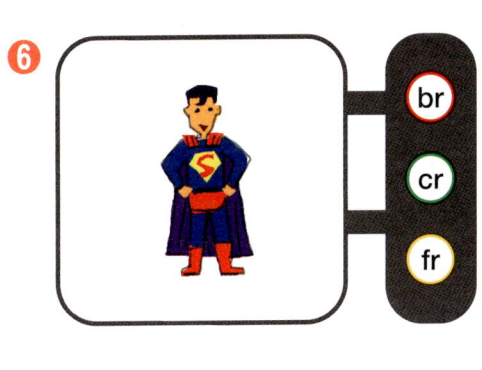

br
cr
fr

Word Search

Circle the words and complete the story.

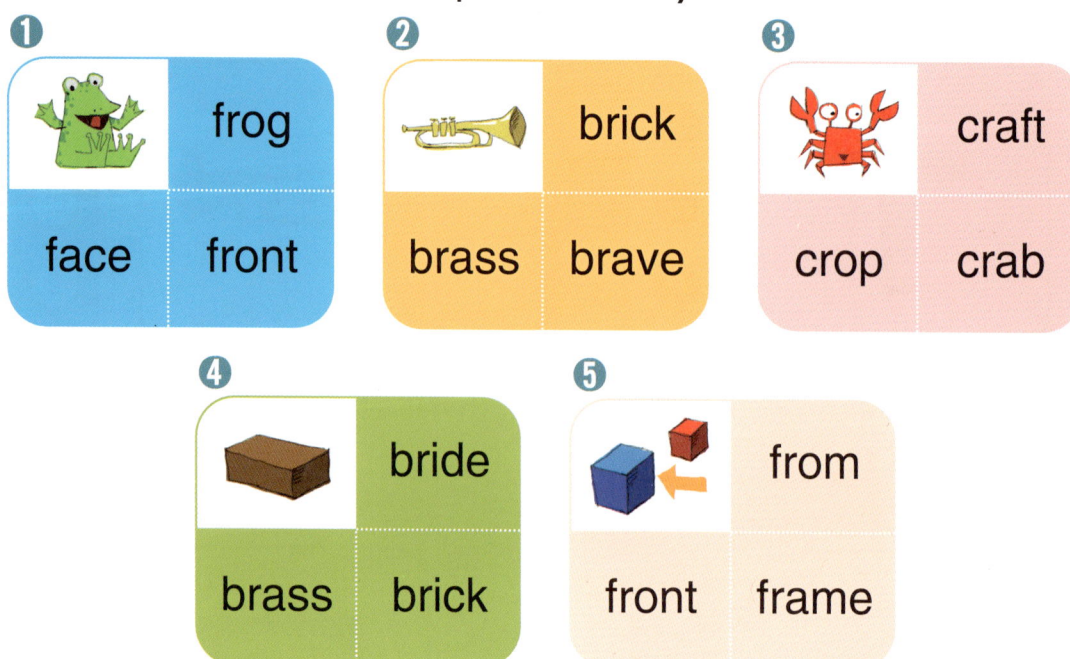

- A ![crab] _____ weds a ![frog] _____.

- The ![crab] _____ is on the red ![brick] _____.

- The ![frog] _____ is on the blue block.

- The ![crab] _____ ![bride] _____ is in a white dress.

- They cut the cake with a blade.

- The ![trumpet] _____ band plays music in ![blocks] _____ of them.

Activity *chant*

How far can the frog jump?
The frog jumps over the block.

How far can the kid jump?
The kid jumps over the brick.

How far can the lion jump?
The lion jumps over the flame.

How far can you jump?
I jump over the net with a pole.

Unit 3 Double Letters gl sl pl

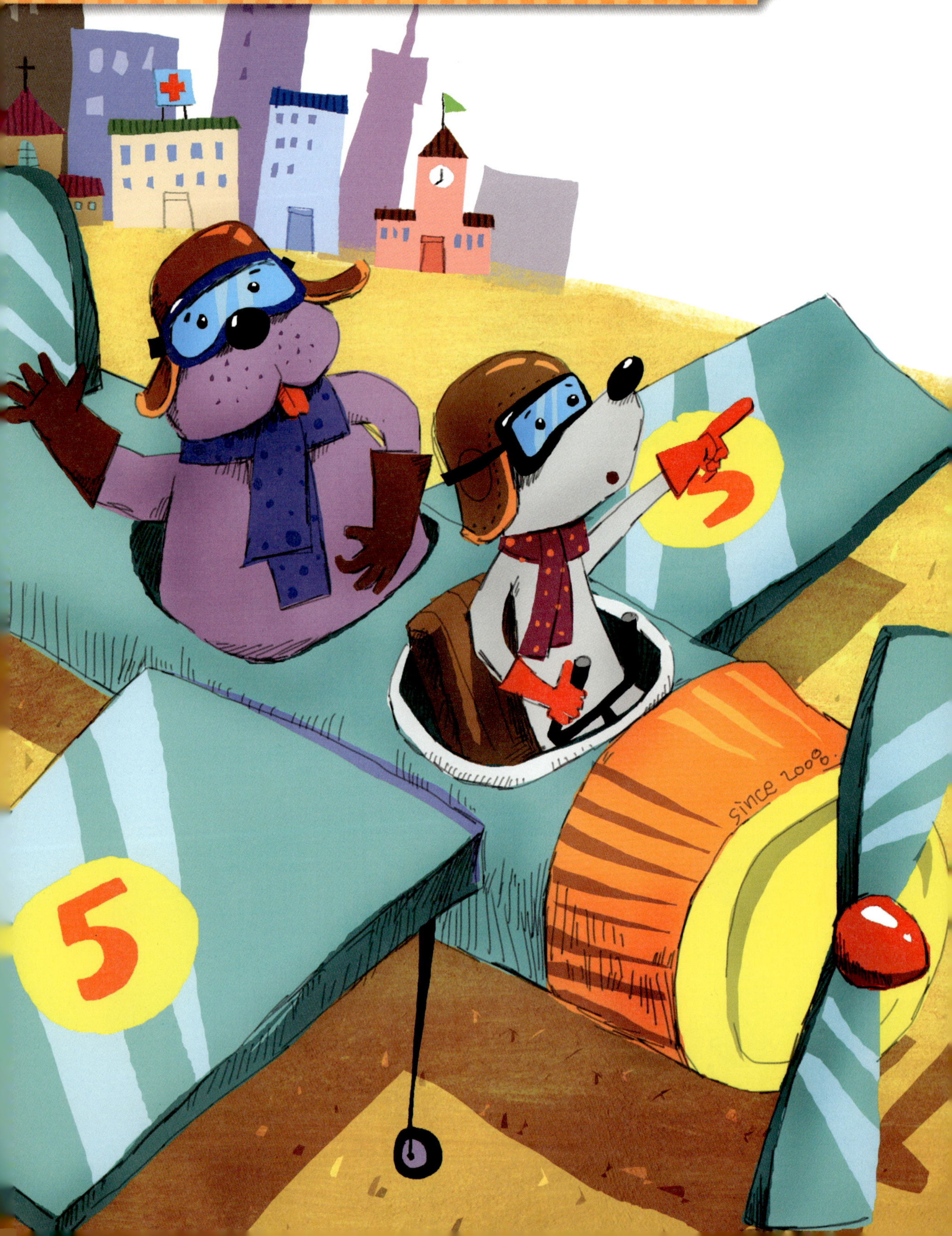

The dogs look at the plane.
They hope to fly in the sky
like the plane.
They plan to make a glider fly.
They make a nice glider
with glue and glass.
But it doesn't fly up to the sky.
One dog is slim;
the other dog is fat.

Sounds

Listen and repeat.

Match and write.

28

Listen, point and repeat.

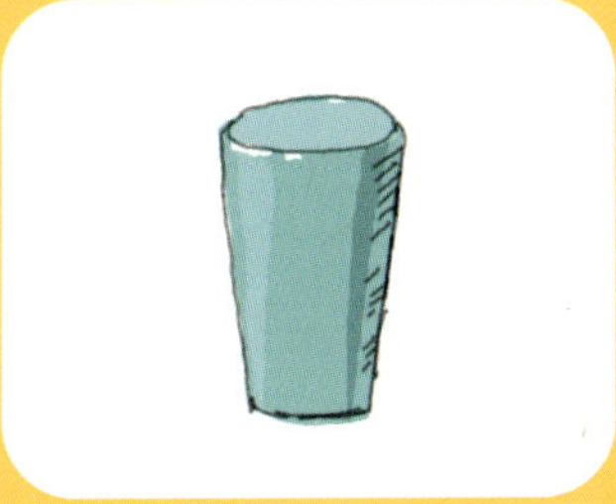

glass

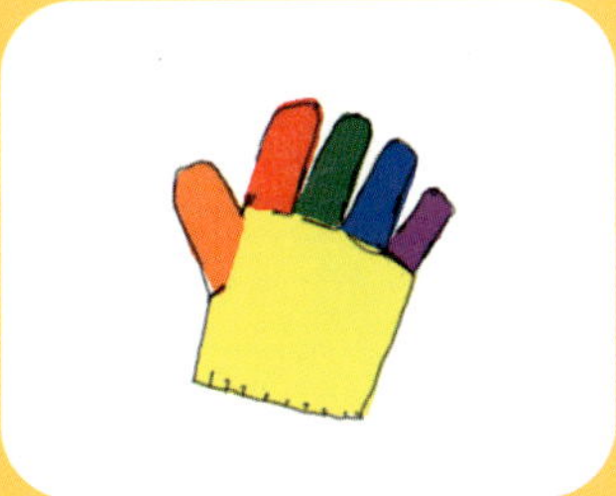

glove

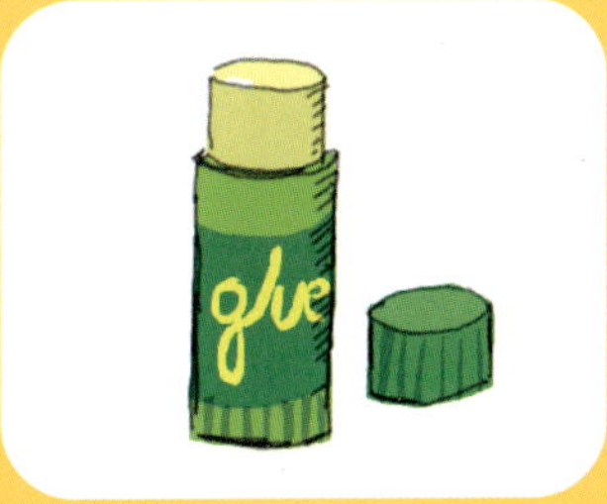

glue

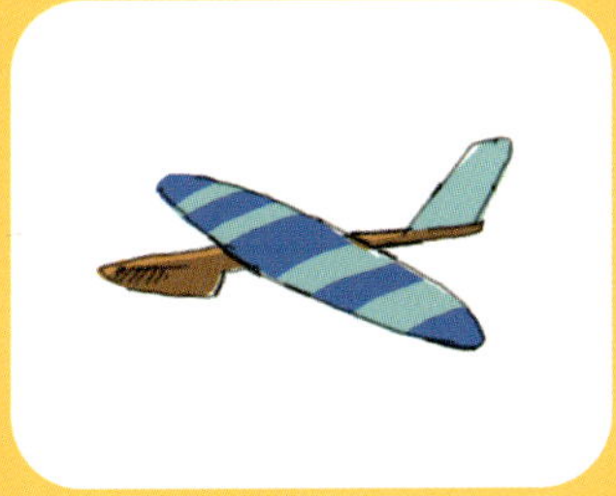

glider

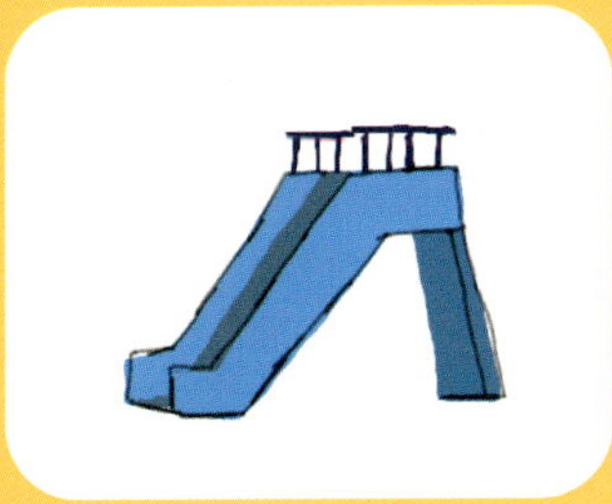

slide

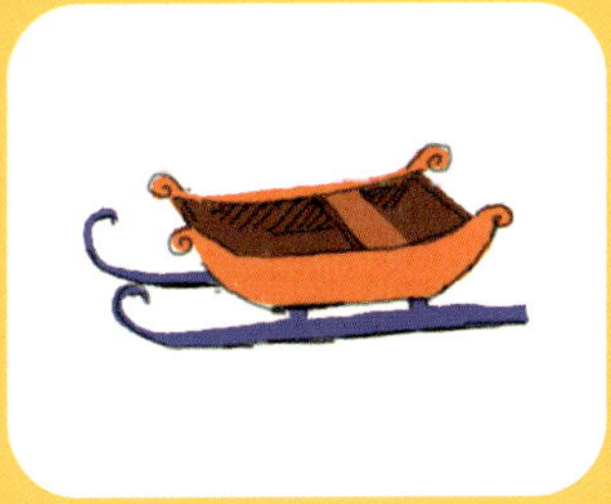

sled

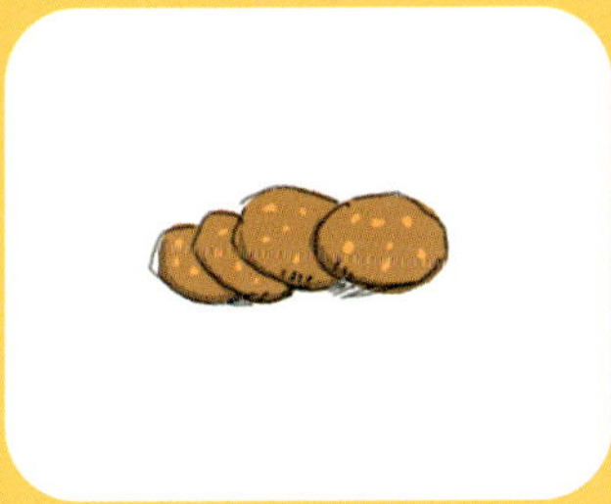

slice

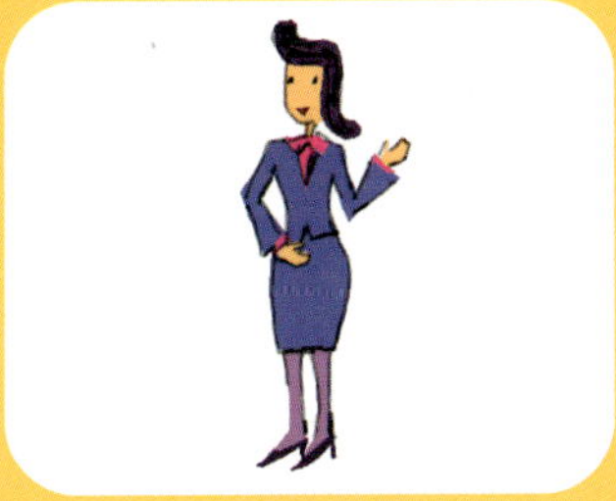

slim

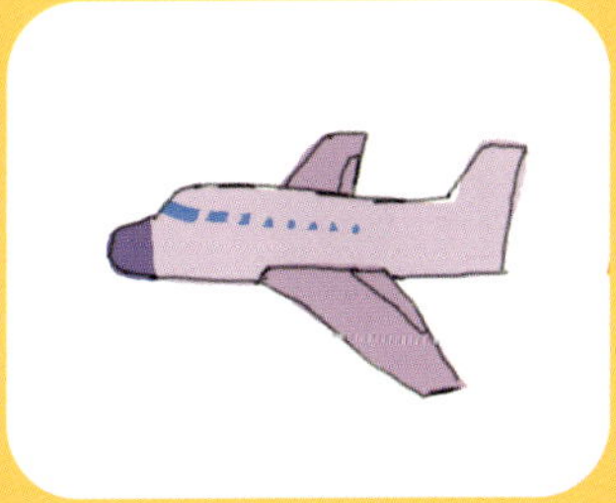

plane

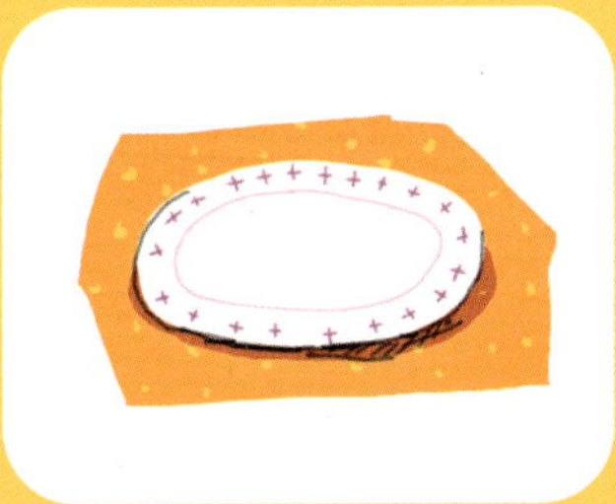

plate

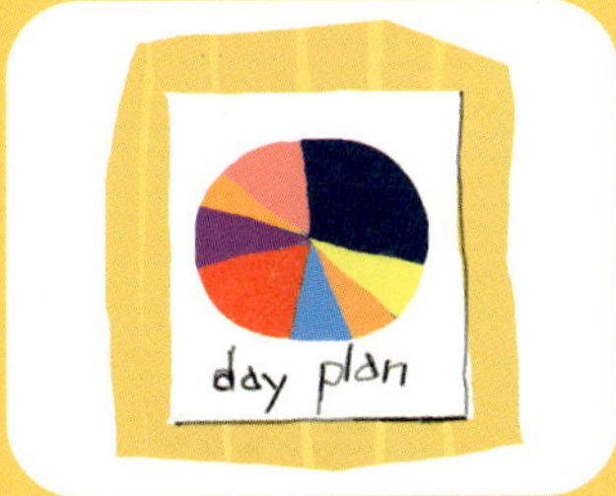

plan

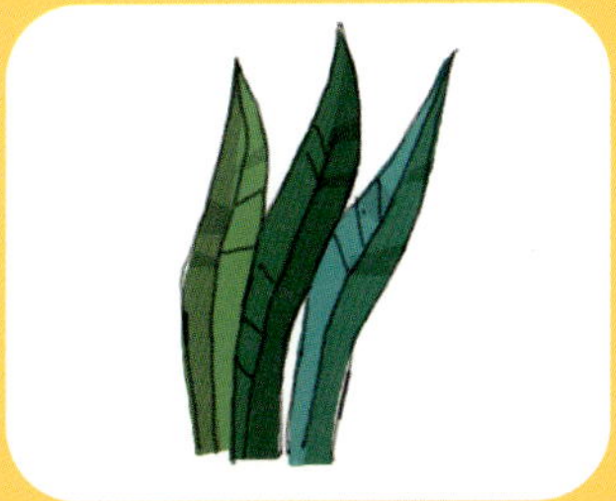

plant

Circle the correct picture for the beginning sound.

1 gl

2 sl

3 pl

Listen, circle and write.

1

_____ ove

2

_____ ed

3

_____ ant

4

_____ im

5

_____ ass

6

_____ ate

7

_____ ide

8

_____ ue

Read and find the correct sentence for the picture.

1

ⓐ The cat has a glue. ☐

ⓑ The cat has gloves. ☐

2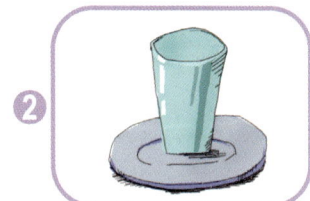

ⓐ The glass is on the plate. ☐

ⓑ The glue is on the plate. ☐

3

ⓐ The kids slice the cake. ☐

ⓑ The kids sit on the slide. ☐

4

ⓐ The pup is in front of the plant. ☐

ⓑ The pup is in front of the plane. ☐

5

ⓐ The fox is slim and the pig is fat. ☐

ⓑ The fox is fat and the pig is slim. ☐

6

ⓐ Frogs ride a slide one by one. ☐

ⓑ Frogs all ride a sled together. ☐

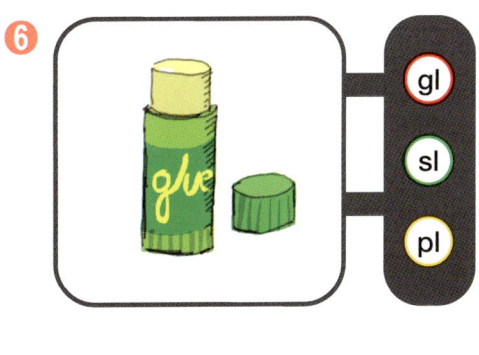

Practice – Write

Color the beginning sound and write the word.

1
gl
sl
pl

2
gl
sl
pl

3
gl
sl
pl

4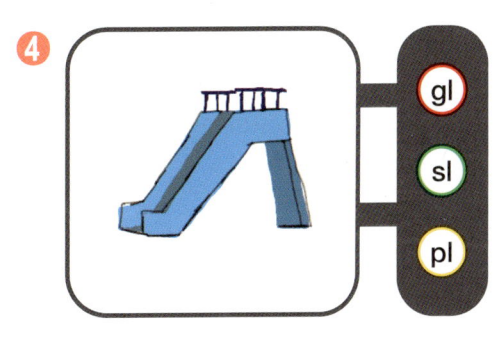
gl
sl
pl

5
gl
sl
pl

6
gl
sl
pl

33

Word Search

Circle the words and complete the story.

①
glider

plate | slide

②
glue

glass | glove

③
plane

plant | plan

④
slice

slide | slim

⑤
glue

plan | sled

⑥
plan

plate | plant

- The dogs look at the _____ .

- They hope to fly in the sky like the _____ .

- They _____ to make a glider fly.

- They make a nice glider with _____ and _____ .

- But it doesn't fly up to the sky.

- One dog is _____ ; the other dog is fat.

Activity *chant*

There are five pairs of gloves.
What are dad's gloves?
The gloves with a plane.
What are mom's gloves?
The gloves with a plant.
What are brother's gloves?
The gloves with a glider.

What are the pup's gloves?
The gloves with a plate.
What are your gloves?
The gloves with a slide.

A frog falls into a trap.
Grass hides the trap.
The frog plays the drum.
A prince traces the drum sound.
The prince gives
the frog a grapevine.
The frog grabs it
and gets out of the trap.

Sounds

Listen and repeat.

Match and write.

Listen, point and repeat.

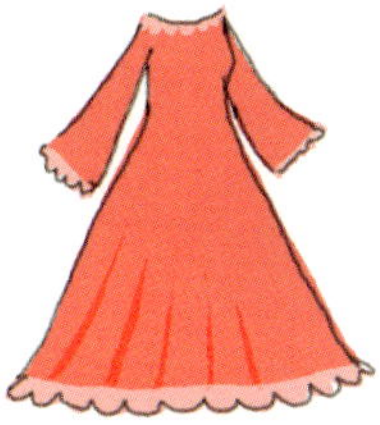

d**r**ess

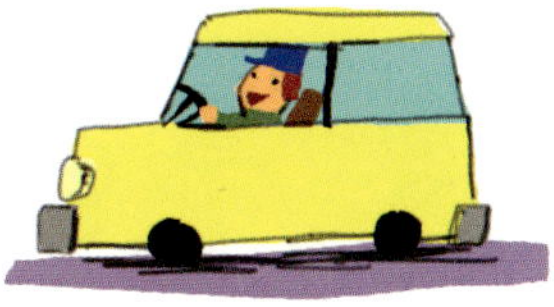

d**r**ive

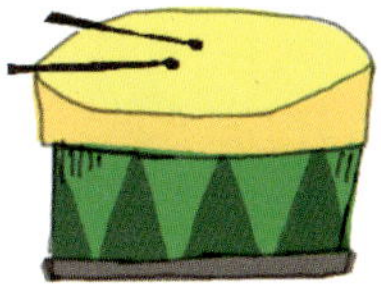

d**r**um

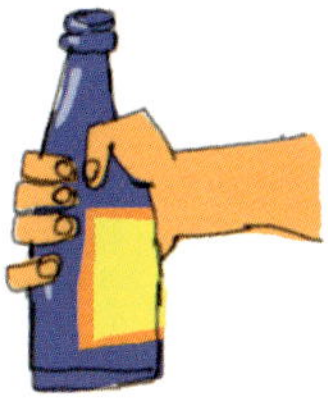

g**r**ab

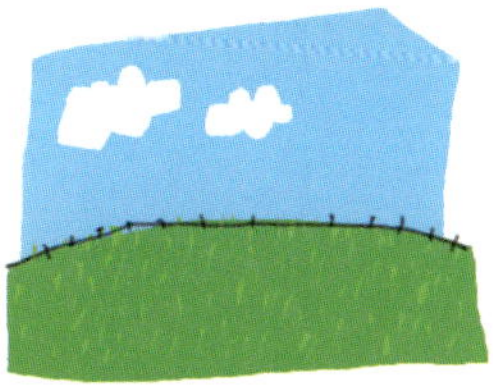

g**r**ass

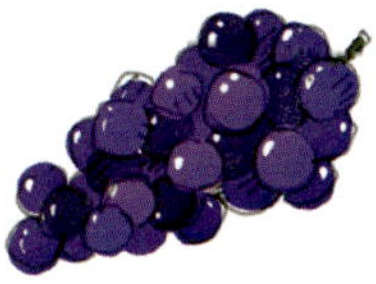

g**r**ape

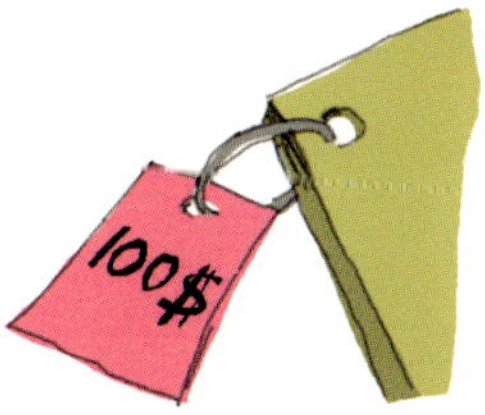

p**r**ice

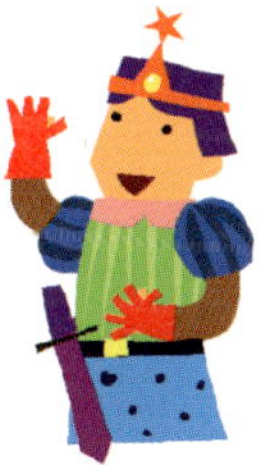

p**r**ince

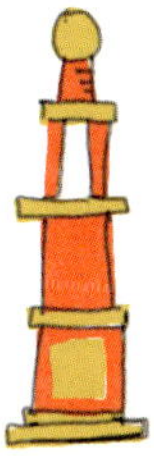

p**r**ize

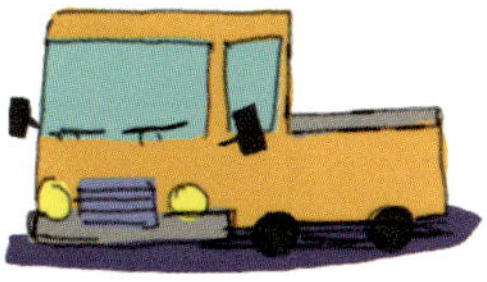

t**r**uck

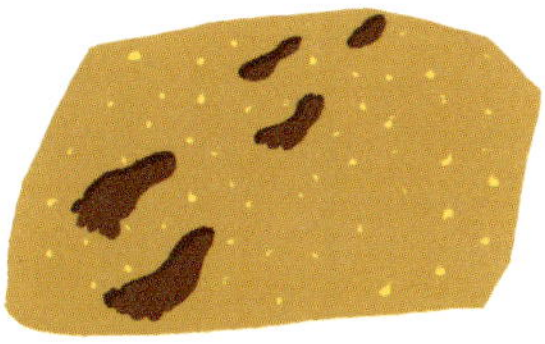

t**r**ace

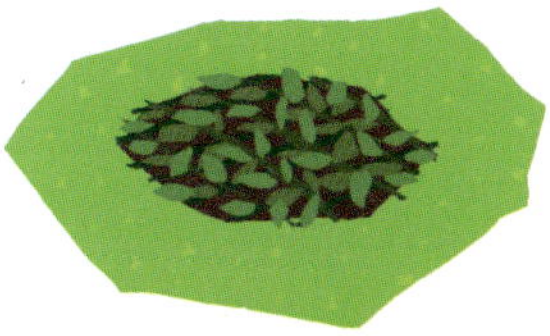

t**r**ap

39

Circle the correct picture for the beginning sound.

❶

❷

❸

❹

Listen, circle and write.

1 _____ ap

2 _____ ize

3 _____ uck

4 _____ ab

5 _____ ass

6 _____ ess

7 _____ ince

8 _____ um

Read and find the correct sentence for the picture.

1

ⓐ The prince plays the drum. ☐

ⓑ The prince drives the truck. ☐

2

ⓐ Dad grabs the plane. ☐

ⓑ Dad grabs the glass. ☐

3

ⓐ The kids get the prize. ☐

ⓑ The kids get the grapes. ☐

4

ⓐ There is a trap under the log. ☐

ⓑ There is a truck in front of the pine. ☐

5

ⓐ The bride has a drum. ☐

ⓑ The bride has grass in the pot. ☐

6

ⓐ The crab traces the slices of ham. ☐

ⓑ The crab puts the prize on the box. ☐

Color the beginning sound and write the word.

1  dr / gr / pr

2  dr / pr / tr

3  dr / gr / pr

4 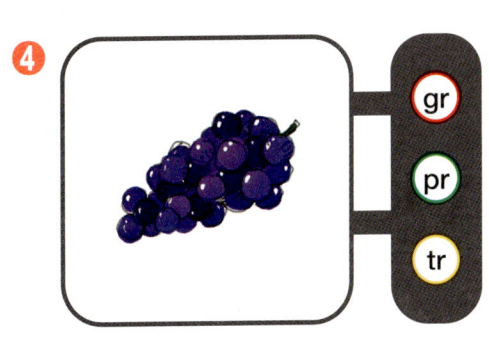 gr / pr / tr

5  dr / pr / tr

6 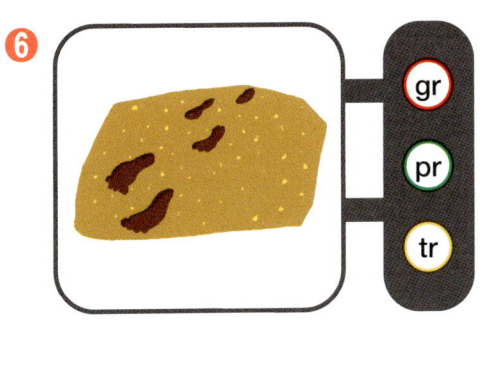 gr / pr / tr

Circle the words and complete the story.

- A frog falls into a _____ .

- _____ hides the _____ .

- The frog plays the _____ .

- A _____ traces the _____ sound.

- The _____ gives the frog a grapevine.

- The frog _____ s it and gets out of the _____ .

Activity *chant*

What word do you find?
from or drum?
I find dr dr drum.
What word do you find?
flame or frame?
I find fr fr frame.
What word do you find?
brass or grass?
I find gr gr grass.
What word do you find?
crab or grab?
I find gr gr grab.

Complete the word.

br   pl   tr   cl   gr   pr   cr   fl

- -

1

P r i z e

2

( ) ( ) a s s

3

( ) ( ) o s s

4

( ) ( ) a m e

5

( ) ( ) u c k

6

( ) ( ) i d e

Find and write different things.

1 gr_ape_

2 gl_____

3 pr_____

4 tr _____

5 bl_____

6 fr _____

1 cl_____

2 cr_____

3 br_____

4 pl_____

5 fr _____

6 fl _____

Listen and catch the word fish.

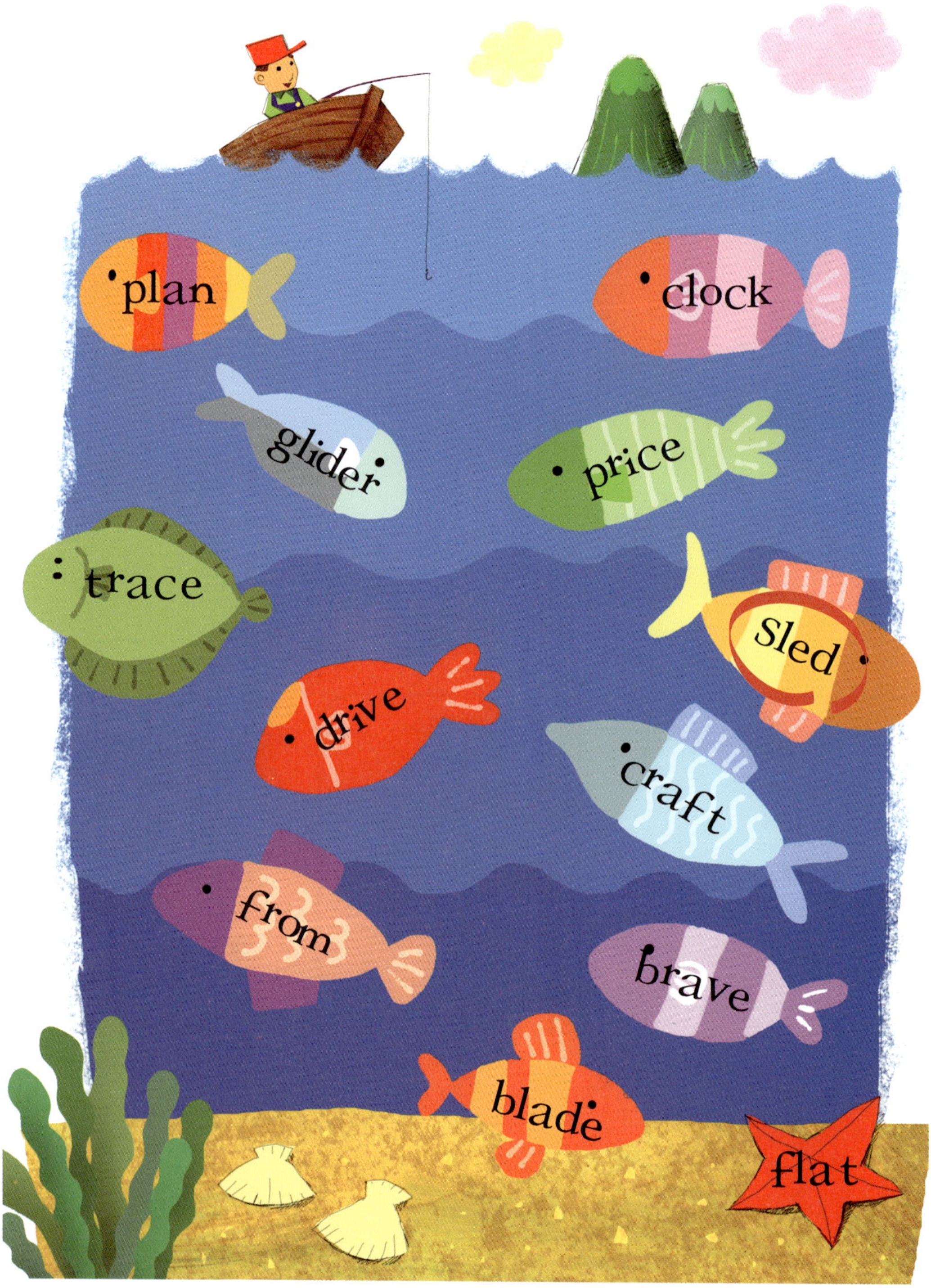

plan

clock

glider

price

trace

Sled

drive

craft

from

brave

blade

flat

Listen, write and match.

1 The prince plays the _drum_.

2 The vase is on the _____.

3 The _____ is on the blue gate.

4 Frogs ride a _____ one by one.

5 The kids pile the _____ blocks.

6 The cat has _____s.

It's time for snacks.
A frog, a crab and a snake have
some sweet cake.
"Can you skate?" asks the frog.
"No, I can't," says the snake.
"Can you ski?" asks the crab.
"No, I can't, but I can swim," says
the snake with a smile.

Sounds

Listen and repeat.

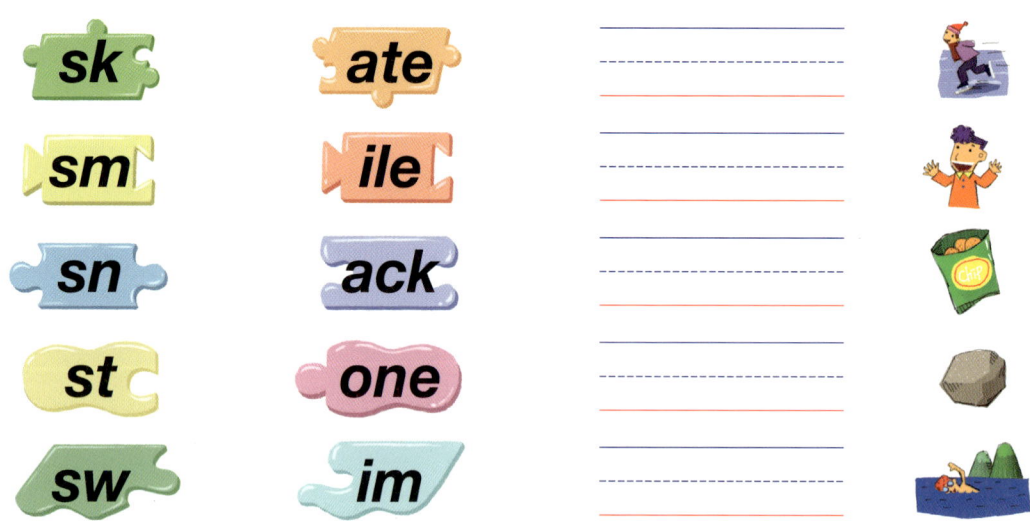

sk	ate	_____	
sm	ile	_____	
sn	ack	_____	
st	one	_____	
sw	im	_____	

Match and write.

st	ack	_____	
sm	im	_____	
sk	one	_____	
sw	ate	_____	
sn	ile	_____	

52

New words

words

Listen, point and repeat.

ski	skate	swim
sweet	snack	snake
smile	smoke	smell
 stop	stone	stove

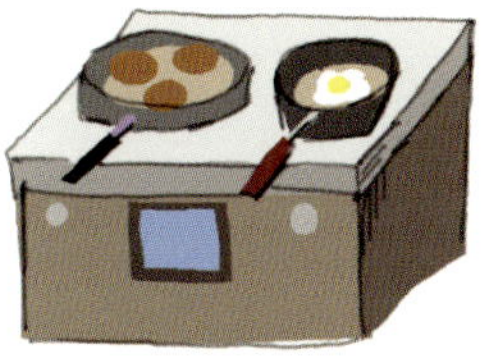

Practice

Circle the correct picture for the beginning sound.

1

2

3

4

5

Listen, circle and write.

①

sn _____

②

sm _____

③

sk _____

④

st _____

⑤

sw _____

⑥

sm _____

⑦

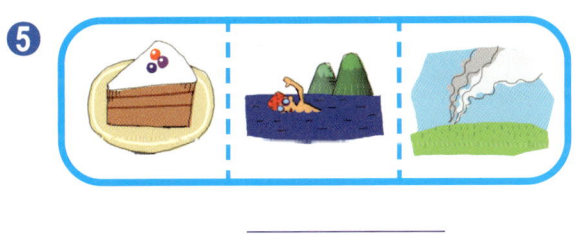

st _____

⑧

sk _____

Read and find the correct sentence for the picture.

ⓐ The men ski on the slope. ☐

ⓑ The men skate on the ice. ☐

ⓐ The frog swims in the lake. ☐

ⓑ The frog skates on the lake. ☐

ⓐ The sweet cake is on the plate. ☐

ⓑ The snacks are on the stove. ☐

ⓐ The black pot is on the stove. ☐

ⓑ The blue pot is on the stone. ☐

ⓐ The snake is on the grass. ☐

ⓑ The smoke come from the truck. ☐

ⓐ The bride smiles at the prince. ☐

ⓑ The bride smells at the rose. ☐

Color the beginning sound and write the word.

1  st / sk / sn

2  st / sn / sw

3  sk / sn / st

4  sm / sn / sw

5  sm / sk / st

6  st / sk / sw

Circle the words and complete the story.

①		②		③	
	ski		swim		snack
swim	skate	smile	sweet	snake	smoke

④		⑤		⑥	
	stone		snake		stove
ski	swim	smoke	skate	skate	smell

- It's time for _____s.

- A frog, a crab and a snake have some _____ cake.

- "Can you _____?" asks the frog.

- "No, I can't," says the _____.

- "Can you _____?" asks the crab.

- "No, I can't, but I can _____," says the snake with a smile.

Acti**vity** *chant*

Quiz time! Quiz time!
What is it?
What is it?

Can Can Can it ski?
Yes, it can.
Yes, it can.

Can Can Can it skate?
No, it can't.
No, it can't.

Can Can Can it swim?
Yes, it can.
Yes, it can.

Can Can Can you guess?
What is it?
What is it?

It's a dog. It's a dog.
It's a dog, dog, dog.

There are three ducks in the lake.
One duck has pink wings.
Another duck has a long neck.
The other duck sings
with a quack-quack.
The king likes the singing duck best.
The king gives the duck a gold ring.

Sounds

Listen and repeat.

ki **ng** 

i **nk** 

du **ck** 

Match and write.

i • • ng • • 

ki • • ck • • 

du • • nk • • 

Listen, point and repeat.

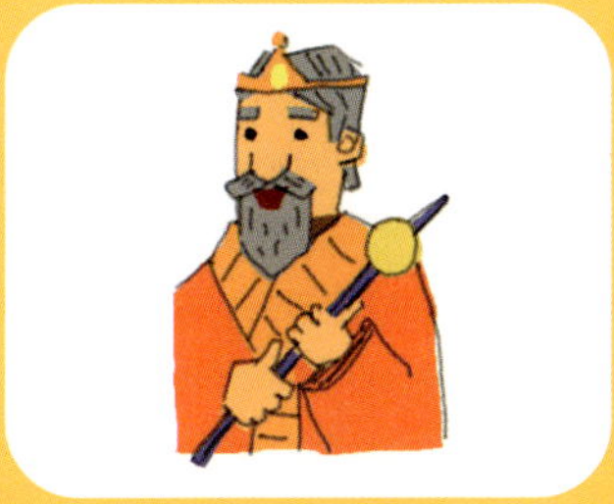

Ki**ng**	ri**ng**	si**ng**
wi**ng**	i**nk**	pi**nk**
si**nk**	dri**nk**	ba**nk**
si**ck**	ne**ck**	du**ck**

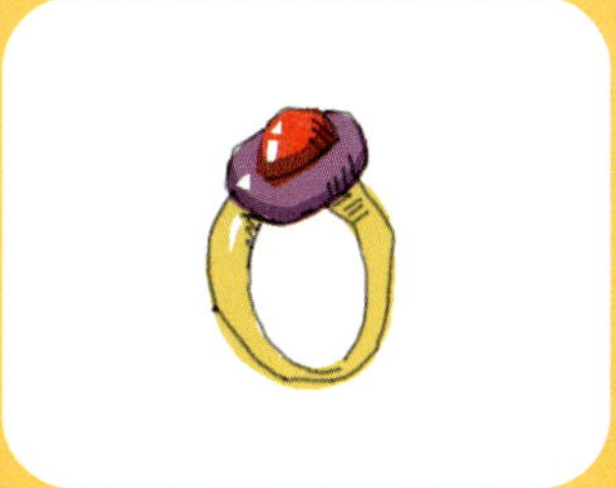

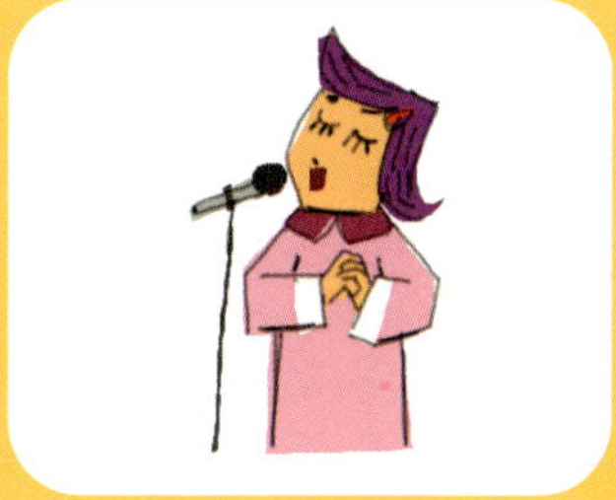

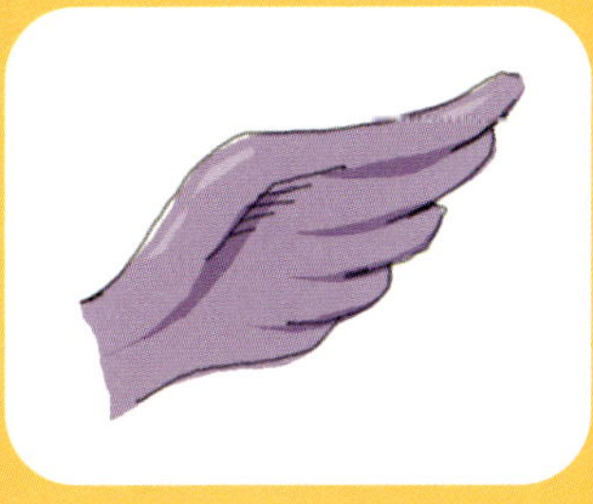

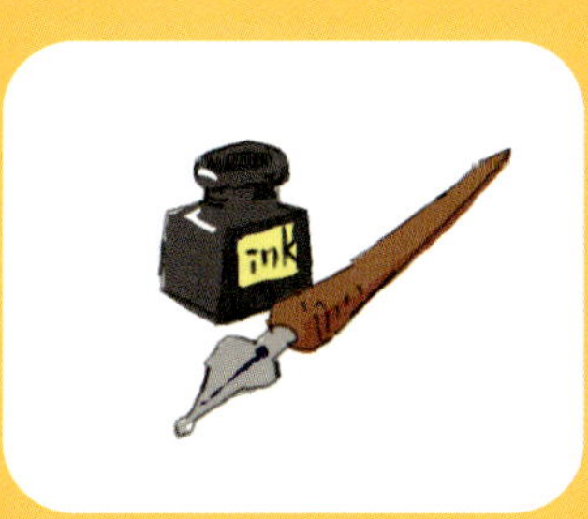

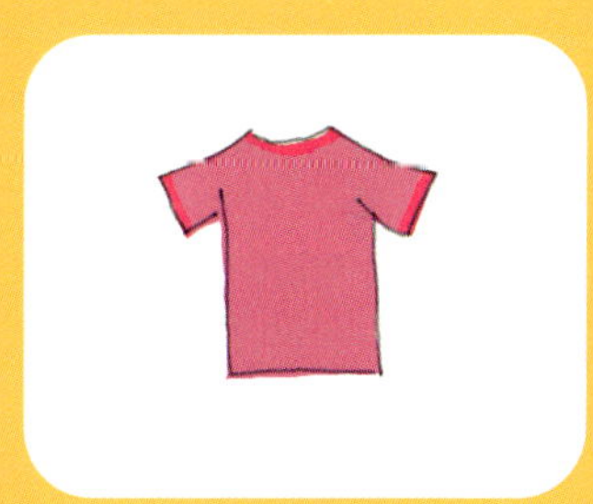

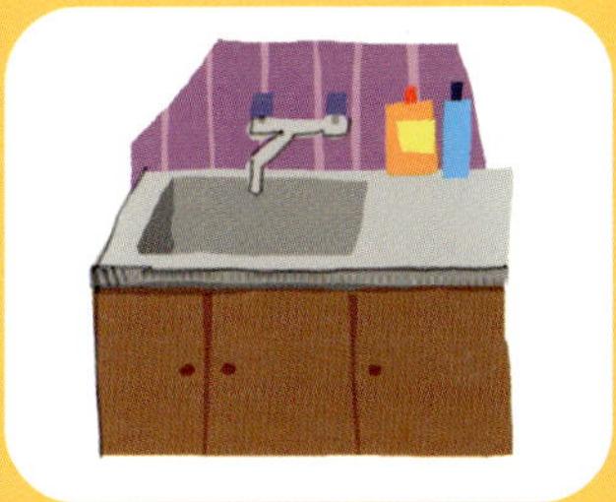

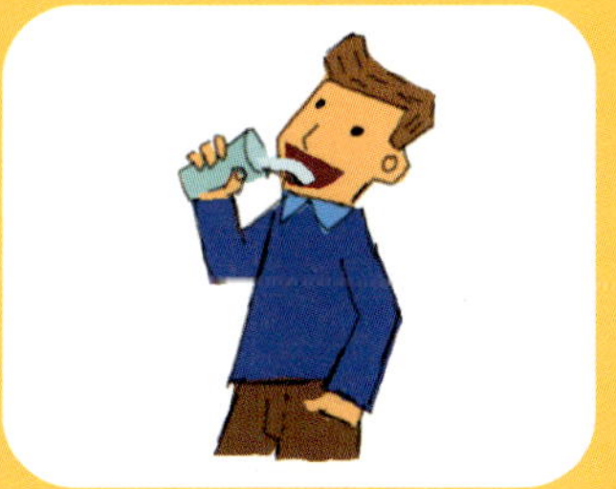

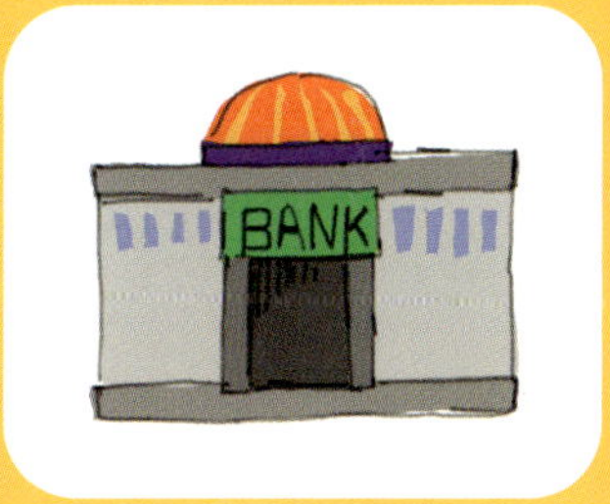

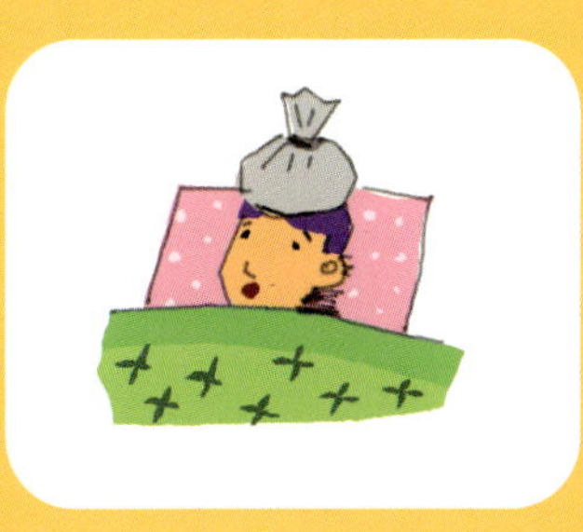

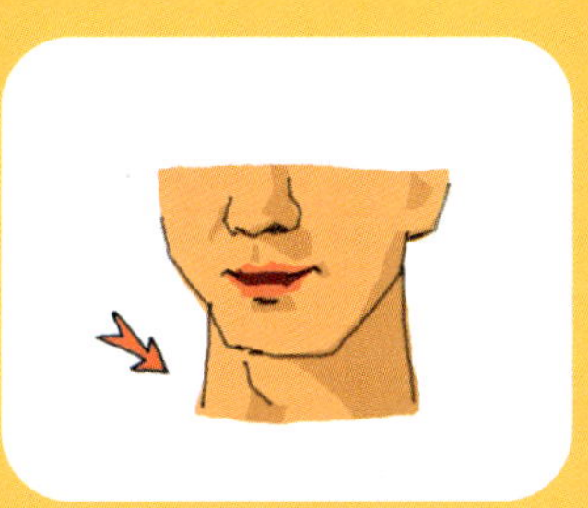

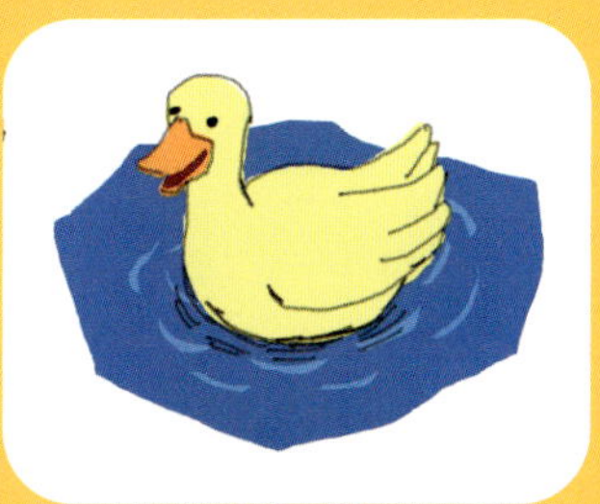

63

Circle the correct picture for the ending sound.

1

nk				

2

3

ng				

Listen, circle and write.

1

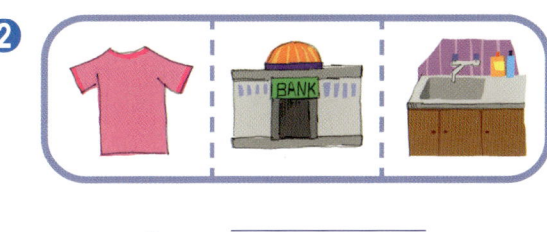

wi _____

2

ba _____

3

du _____

4

si _____

5

ri _____

6

pi _____

7

ne _____

8

dri _____

Practice – Read

Read and find the correct sentence for the picture.

1

ⓐ The ink is on the drum. ☐

ⓑ The ink is on the dress. ☐

2

ⓐ The duck has pink wings. ☐

ⓑ The duck has a pink ring. ☐

3

ⓐ The kid sings with a duck. ☐

ⓑ The kid sings at the bank. ☐

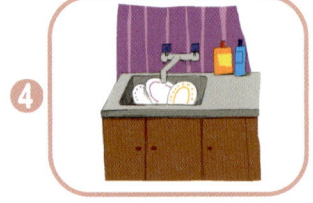

4

ⓐ The plates are in the sink. ☐

ⓑ The plate is under the duck. ☐

5

ⓐ The king has a blue ring. ☐

ⓑ The king has a blue wing. ☐

6

ⓐ The ducks drink with a hose. ☐

ⓑ The dogs drink with a hose. ☐

Color the ending sound and write the word.

1

- ng
- nk
- ck

_____

2

- ng
- nk
- ck

_____

3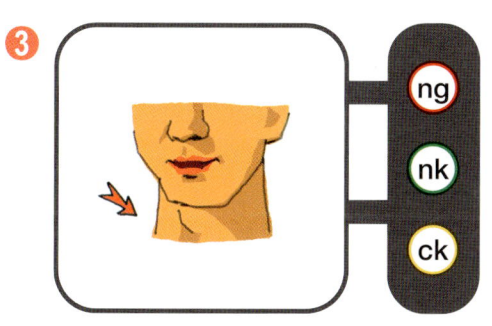

- ng
- nk
- ck

_____

4

- ng
- nk
- ck

_____

5

- ng
- nk
- ck

_____

6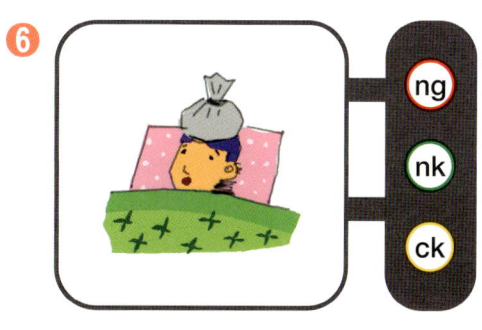

- ng
- nk
- ck

_____

Circle the words and complete the story.

- There are three  _____s in the lake.

- One _____ has pink wings.

- Another _____ has a long _____.

- The other _____ _____s with a quack-quack.

- The king likes the _____ing _____ best.

- The king gives the duck a gold ring.

Activity *chant*

The duck has wings.
Flap flap flap wings.
The man has rings.
Toss toss toss the rings.
The prince is with the king.
Sing sing sing for him.
The kid has some ink.
Write write write the letter.

The little chick gets
some chips and chocolate.
The chip has a ship shape.
The chocolate has a bench shape.
The little chick has all the snacks.
Mom hen says, "You should wash
your hands and brush your teeth."
The little chick says, "Yes, mom."

Listen and repeat.

 sh   ip

 bru   sh

 ch   ick

 ben   ch

Match and write.

ben   •   • ick

ch   •   • ch

sh   •   • ip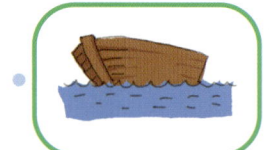

bru   •   • sh

72

Listen, point and repeat.

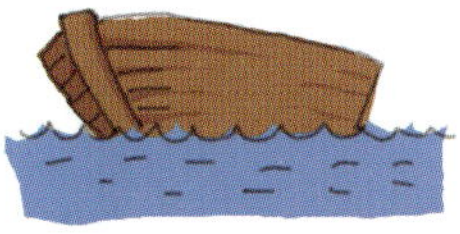

ship	**sh**op	**sh**ape
bru**sh**	wa**sh**	di**sh**
chick	**ch**ip	**ch**ocolate
ben**ch**	ri**ch**	**ch**ur**ch**

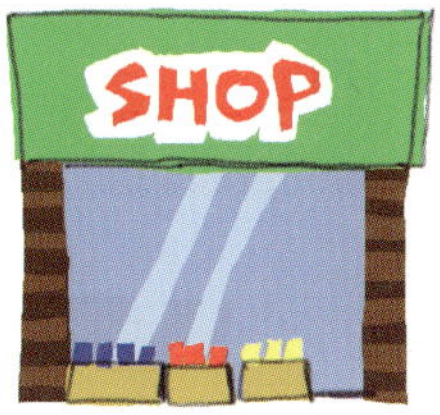

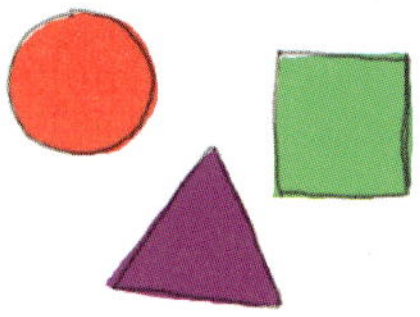

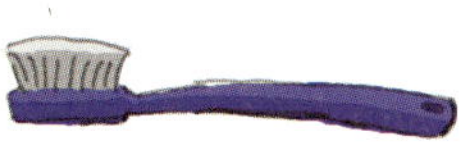

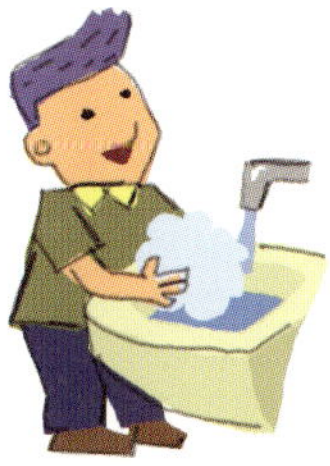

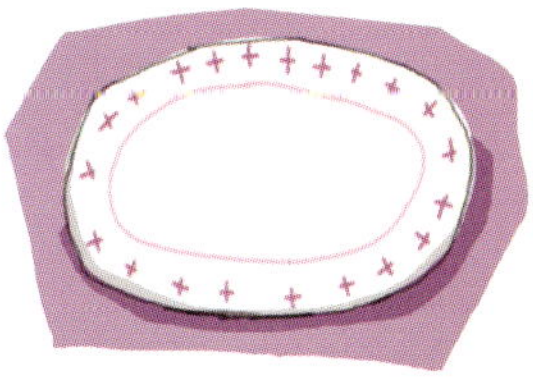

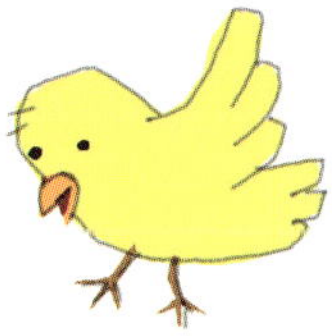

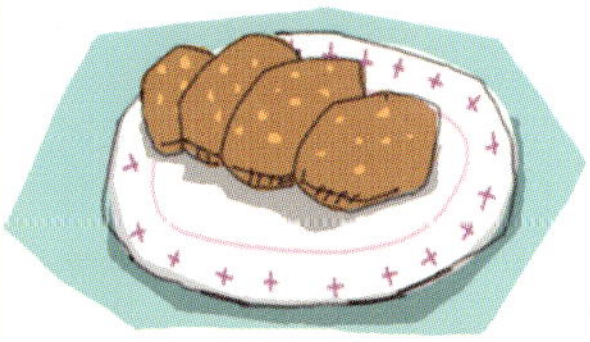

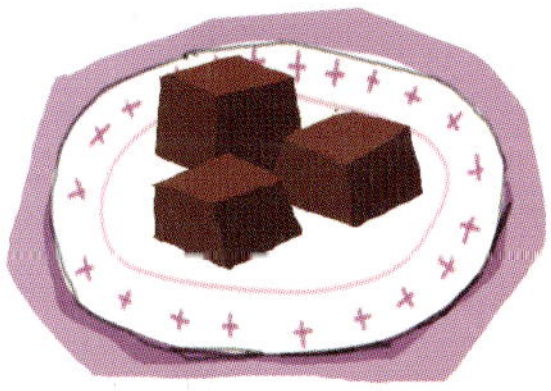

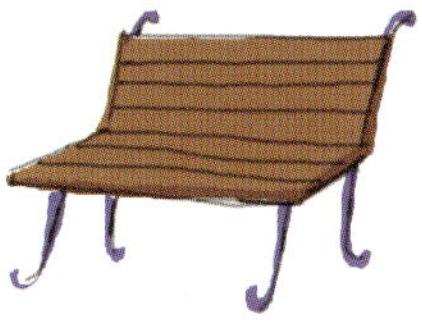

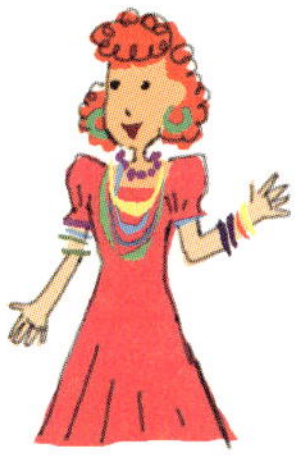

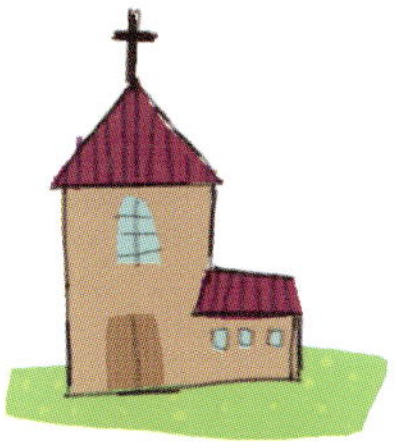

73

Practice

Circle the correct picture for the sound.

1

sh_

2

ch_

3

_ch

4

_sh

Listen, circle and write.

1

op

2

wa

3

ick

4

ip

5

ben

6

ip

7

di

8

bru

Practice – Read

Read and find the correct sentence for the picture.

1
ⓐ The rich king has a big ship. ☐
ⓑ The rich king has a big shop. ☐

2
ⓐ The chicks wash the dish. ☐
ⓑ The chicks brush the bench. ☐

3
ⓐ The kid has chips. ☐
ⓑ The kid has chocolate. ☐

4
ⓐ The bench is in front of the church. ☐
ⓑ The bench is in front of the shop. ☐

5
ⓐ The shape of the chip is a ring. ☐
ⓑ The shape of the ship is a fish. ☐

6
ⓐ The chick is on the bench. ☐
ⓑ The chick is in the sink. ☐

Color the sound and write the word.

1

2
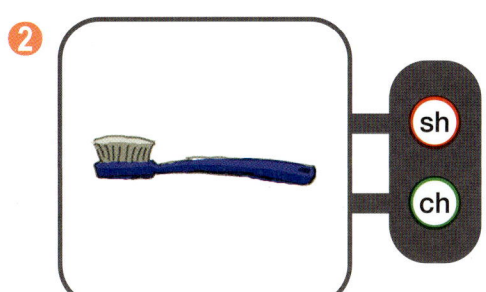

3
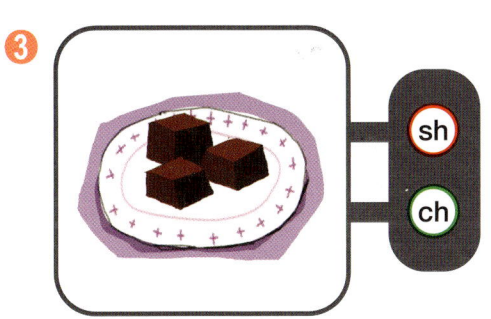

4

5

6

Word Search

Circle the words and complete the story.

- The little _____ gets some _____s and chocolate.

- The _____ has a _____ _____.

- The chocolate has a bench _____.

- The little _____ has all the snacks.

- Mom hen says, "You should _____ your hands

  and _____ your teeth."

- The little _____ says, "Yes, mom."

78

Activity *chant*

I wash my hands.
Good night, mom.
Good night, mom.
-And wash your face.
I wash my face.
Good night, mom.
Good night, mom.
-And btush your teeth.

I brush my teeth.
Good night, mom.
Good night, mom.
-And Sweet dreams, honey.

A whale has big teeth.
But the whale hurts his thumbs.
The whale can't brush his teeth.
The thin fish whispers to the crab.
They help the whale brush his teeth
and take a bath.
The whale thinks they are very kind.

Listen and repeat.

 **th**   **in**

ba   **th**   

wh   **ale**   

ph   **oto**

Match and write.

ba   oto   _____   

wh   in   _____   

th   th   _____   

ph   ale   _____   

Listen, point and repeat.

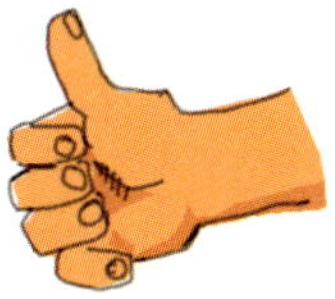

thumb	**th**in	**th**ink
ba**th**	pa**th**	tee**th**
whale	**wh**ite	**wh**isper
whip	**ph**oto	**ph**one

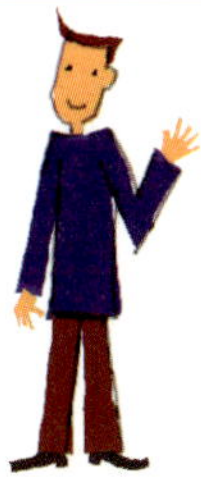

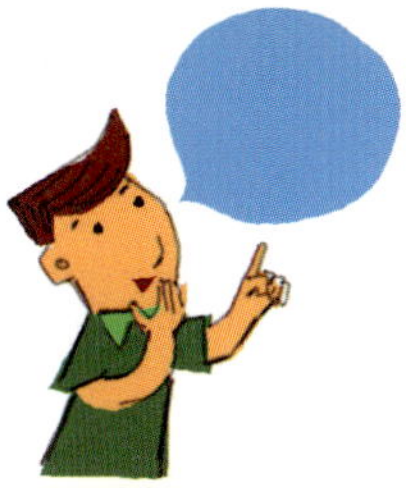

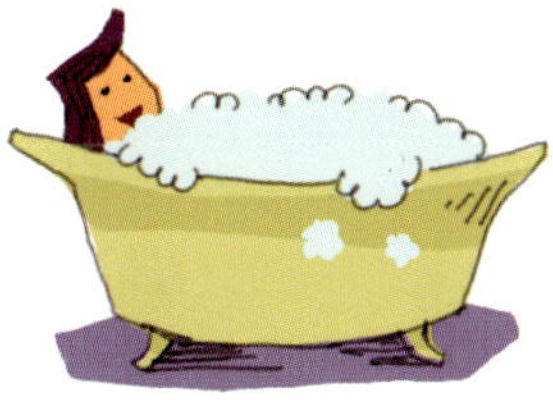

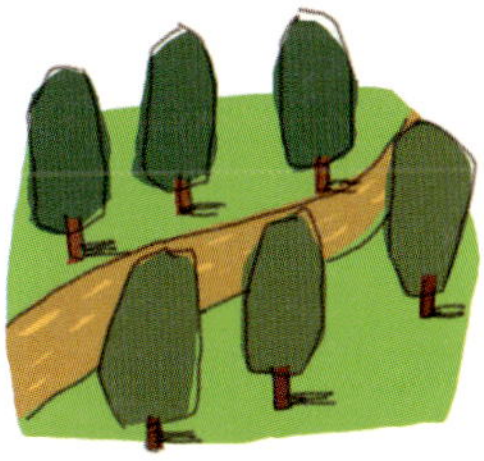

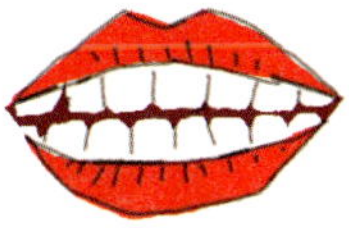

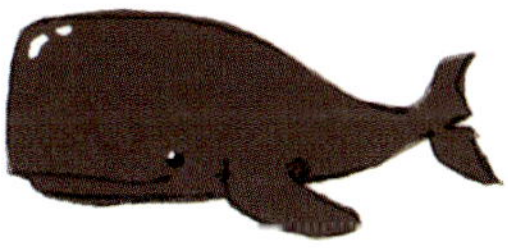

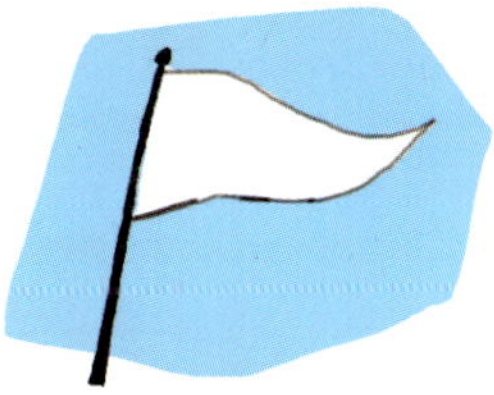

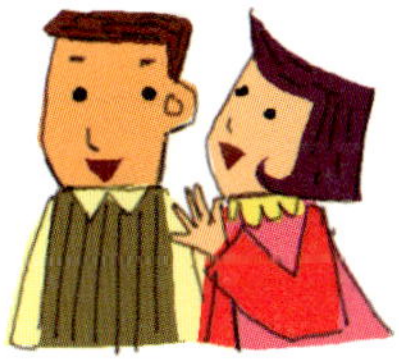

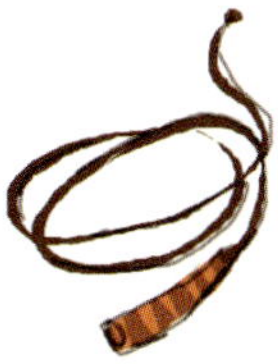

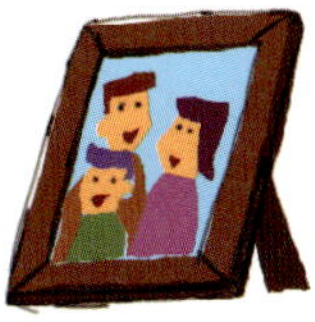

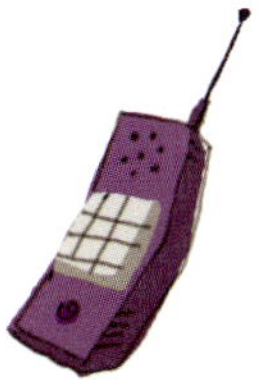

83

Circle the correct picture for the sound.

1

wh

2

_th

3

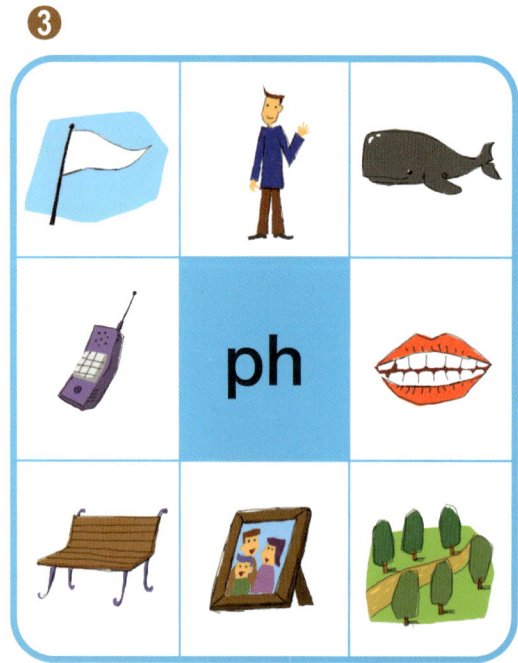

ph

4

th_

Listen, circle and write.

1

tee _____

2

_____ one

3

_____ in

4

_____ ale

5

ba _____

6

_____ umb

7

_____ oto

8

_____ ite

Practice – Read

Read and find the correct sentence for the picture.

1 ⓐ The whale is in the huge waves. ☐

ⓑ The whale has white teeth. ☐

2 ⓐ The kids whisper to mom. ☐

ⓑ The kids think mom is thin. ☐

3 ⓐ The thin man is on the path. ☐

ⓑ The thin man takes a bath. ☐

4 ⓐ The kid hurts his thumb. ☐

ⓑ The rat hurts his teeth. ☐

5 ⓐ The chick has the brush. ☐

ⓑ The chick has the whip. ☐

6 ⓐ The man is on the phone. ☐

ⓑ The man is on the path. ☐

Color the sound and write the word.

1

th
wh
ph

_____
- - - - - - - - - - - - - -
_____

2

th
wh
ph

_____
- - - - - - - - - - - - - -
_____

3

th
wh
ph

_____
- - - - - - - - - - - - - -
_____

4

th
wh
ph

_____
- - - - - - - - - - - - - -
_____

5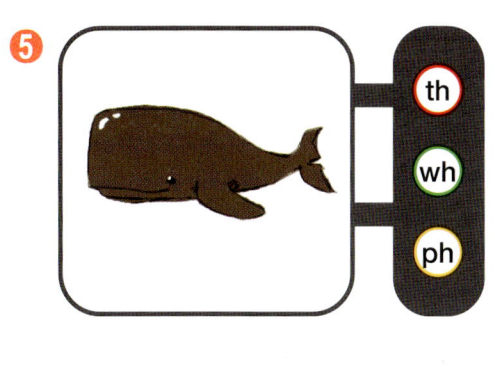

th
wh
ph

_____
- - - - - - - - - - - - - -
_____

6

th
wh
ph

_____
- - - - - - - - - - - - - -
_____

Circle the words and complete the story.

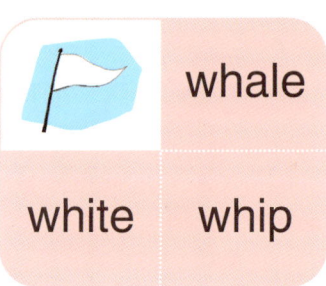

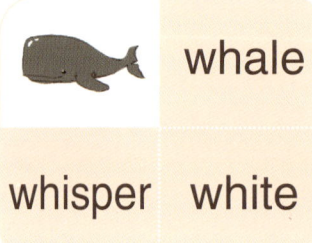

- A _____ has big teeth.

- But the _____ hurts his _____s.

- The _____ can't brush his teeth.

- The _____ fish _____s to the crab.

- They help the _____ brush his teeth

  and take a _____.

- The _____ _____s they are very kind.

88

Activity *chant*

There is the thumb family.
Where are they? What do they do?
Daddy thumb is in the bath.
He takes a bath.
Mommy thumb is on the path.
She takes a walk.
Sister thumb is at the bank.
She is on the phone.
Little thumb is on the whale.
He plays with the whale.

Review 2

Complete the word.

ch   th   ck   st   sh   sn   sw   nk

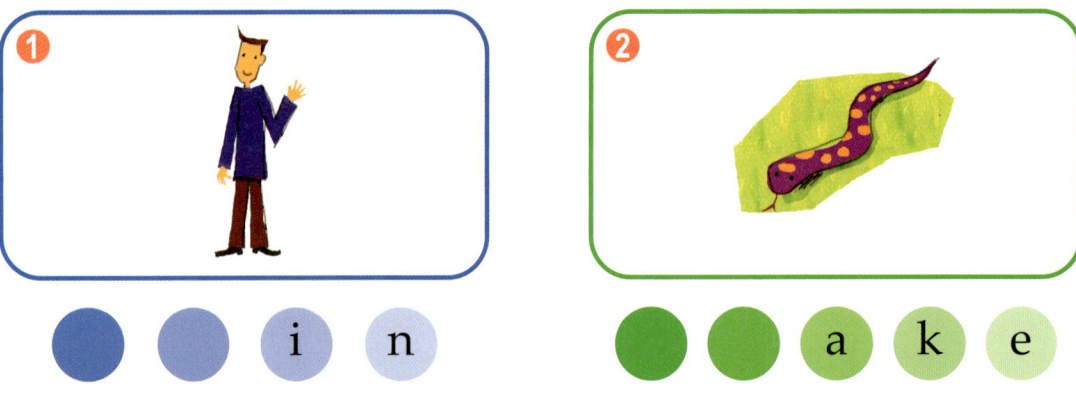

1 ○ ○ i n

2 ○ ○ a k e

3 ○ ○ o p

4 d u ○ ○

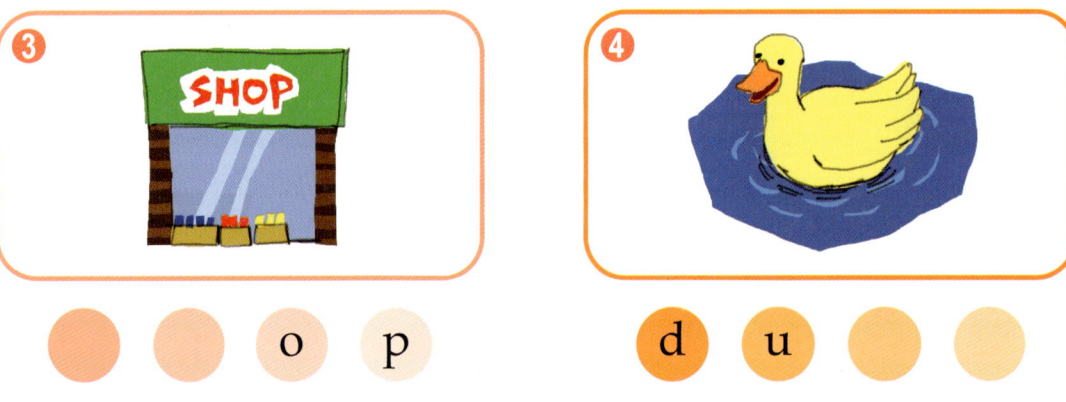

5 ○ ○ i m

6 s i ○ ○

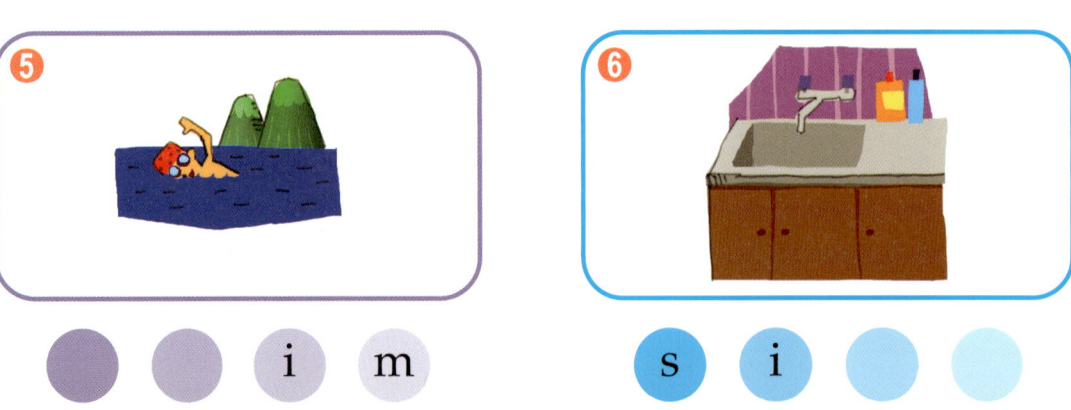

Listen and catch the word bubble.

Find the right sentence for each picture.

❶ The man has gold rings. ☺ ✗ ✓

❷ The chicks flap their wings. ☺ ☹

❸ The man is smiling. ☺ ☹

❹ The bench is in front of the shop. ☺ ☹

❺ The whale swims in the sea. ☺ ☹

❶ The pot is on the stove. 😊 ☹

❷ The ship is in front of the table. 😊 ☹

❸ The photo is on the table. 😊 ☹

❹ The kid with the pink dress has some snacks. 😊 ☹

❺ The glass is in the sink. 😊 ☹

Test

Listen and check.

1

2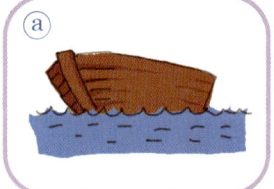

3

4

5

6

7 ng

 ⓐ ✓

 ⓑ

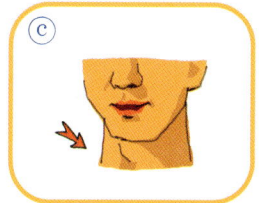 ⓒ

8 st

 ⓐ

 ⓑ

 ⓒ

9 sh

 ⓐ

 ⓑ

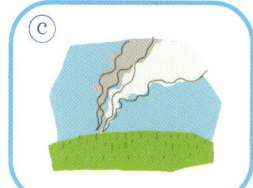 ⓒ

10 th

 ⓐ

 ⓑ

 ⓒ

11 sn

 ⓐ

 ⓑ

 ⓒ

12 wh

 ⓐ

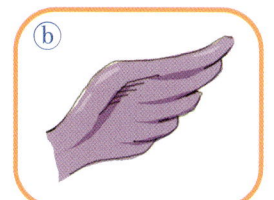 ⓑ

 ⓒ

Test

Listen and write.

1. The _frog_ _swim_ s in the lake.

2. The _____ pot is on the _____.

3. The _____ is on the _____.

4. The _____es are in the _____.

5 The _____ s wash the _____.

6 The _____ of the chip is a _____.

7 The kids _____ to mom.

8 The man is on the _____.

Test

Listen and unscramble.

❶ akSte
skate

❷ Sburh
_____

❸ ikhcc
_____

❹ helaw
_____

❺ muthb
_____

❻ ucdk
_____

98

Circle the words and find the letter.

1

a	f	u	a	t	g
p	l	r	c	v	l
g	a	c	a	p	o
n	m	e	h	m	v
x	e	r	i	m	e
c	l	a	t	a	c

The words are

We can find the letter _____.

2

a	b	a	n	k	e
b	e	s	a	j	d
i	n	e	c	k	y
n	c	o	r	t	i
g	h	l	e	o	m
e	d	f	a	h	p

The words are

We can find the letter _____.

Answer Key

8p

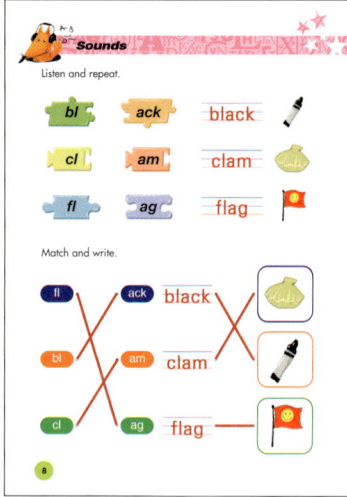

11p

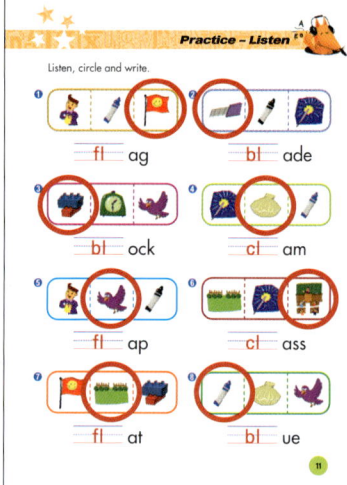

14p

❶ clock
❷ blue
❸ block
❹ flag
❺ black
❻ class

class
black clock
blue block
flag

10p

12p

❷ b
❸ a
❹ a
❺ b
❻ a

13p

❷ fl / flap
❸ fl / flame
❹ cl / clock
❺ bl / block
❻ cl / clap

18p

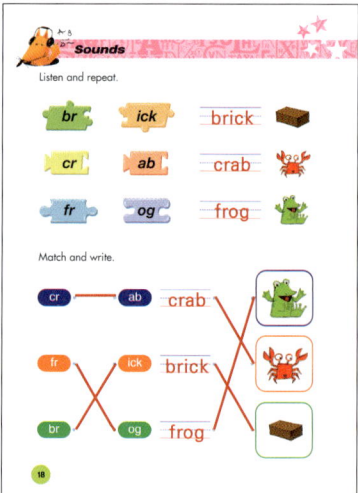

20p

23p

❶ cr / cross

❷ br / brass

❸ br / brick

❹ fr / frame

❺ cr / crab

❻ br / brave

24p

❶ frog

❷ brass

❸ crab

❹ brick

❺ front

crab frog

crab brick

frog

crab bride

brass front

28p

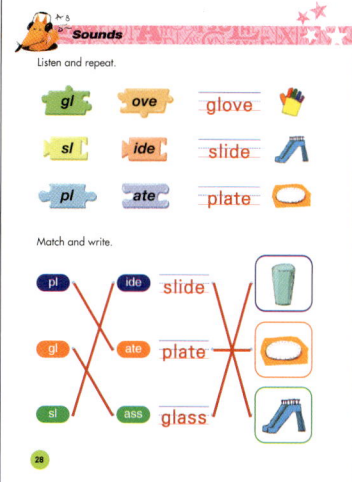

21p

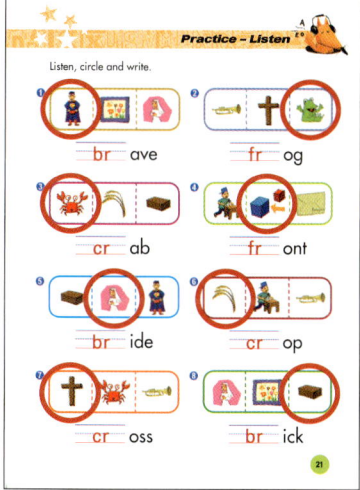

22p

❶ a

❷ a

❸ b

❹ a

❺ b

❻ a

30p

31p

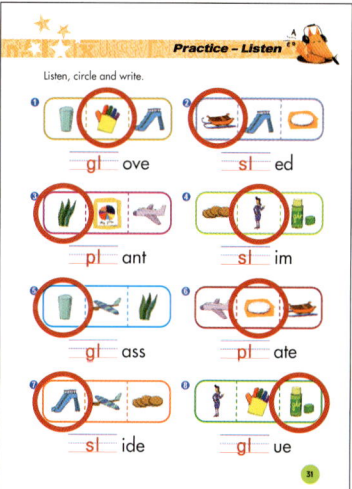

32p

❶ b

❷ a

❸ b

❹ a

❺ a

❻ a

Answer Key

33p
❶ pl / plan
❷ pl / plane
❸ gl / glider
❹ sl / slide
❺ pl / plant
❻ gl / glue

34p
❶ glider
❷ glass
❸ plane
❹ slim
❺ glue
❻ plan

plane
plane
plan
glue glass
slim

38p

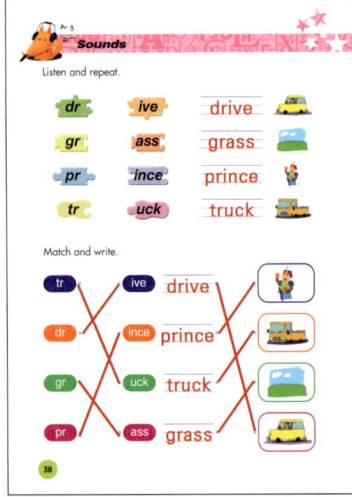

40p

41p

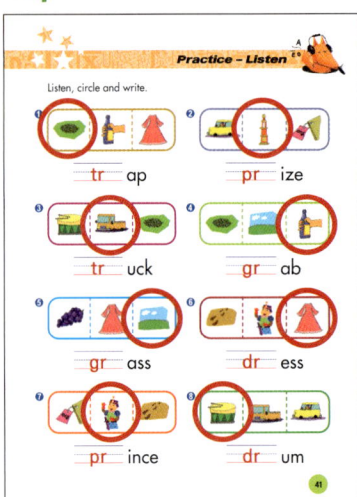

42p
❶ a
❷ b
❸ a
❹ b
❺ b
❻ a

43p
❶ pr / prize
❷ dr / drive
❸ gr / grass
❹ gr / grape
❺ pr / prince
❻ tr / trace

44p
❶ trace
❷ prince
❸ grab
❹ trap
❺ grass
❻ drum

trap
Grass trap
drum
prince drum
prince
grab trap

102

Review1

46p
❶ pr   ❷ cl
❸ cr   ❹ fl
❺ tr   ❻ br

47p
picture A
❶ ape   ❷ ass
❸ ize   ❹ uck
❺ ock   ❻ og

picture B
❶ am   ❷ ab
❸ ick   ❹ ane
❺ ame   ❻ ag

48p
❶ sled
❷ glider
❸ brave
❹ trace
❺ clock
❻ from
❼ drive

49p

Listen, write and match.

❶ The prince plays the **drum**.

❷ The vase is on the **brick**.

❸ The **clock** is on the blue gate.

❹ Frogs ride a **slide** one by one.

❺ The kids pile the **blue** blocks.

❻ The cat has **glove**s.

52p

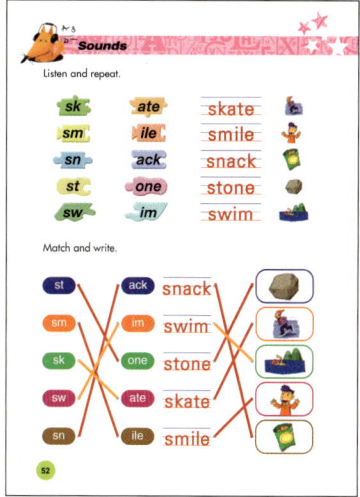

54p

Answer Key

55p

56p

❶ b
❷ a
❸ b
❹ b
❺ a
❻ b

57p

❶ st / stone
❷ sw / sweet
❸ sn / snack
❹ sm / smoke
❺ sk / skate
❻ sw / swim

58p

❶ ski
❷ sweet
❸ snack
❹ swim
❺ snake
❻ skate

snack
sweet
skate
snake
ski
swim

62p

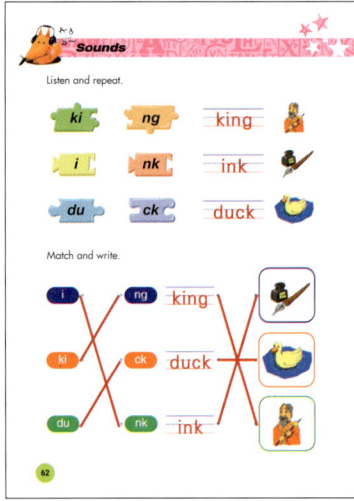

64p

65p

66p

❶ b
❷ b
❸ a
❹ a
❺ b
❻ a

67p

❶ ng / sing
❷ nk / pink
❸ ck / neck
❹ ng / king
❺ nk / sink
❻ ck / sick

68p

❶ sing
❷ duck
❸ ring
❹ neck
❺ wing
❻ pink

duck
duck
duck neck
duck sing
sing duck

72p

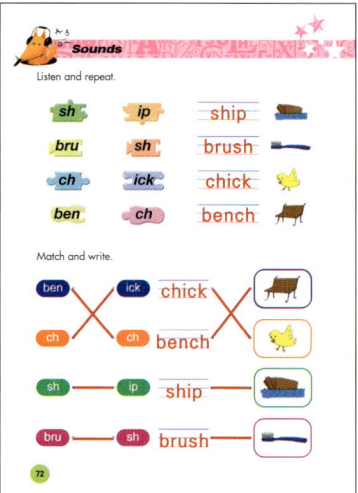

74p

75p

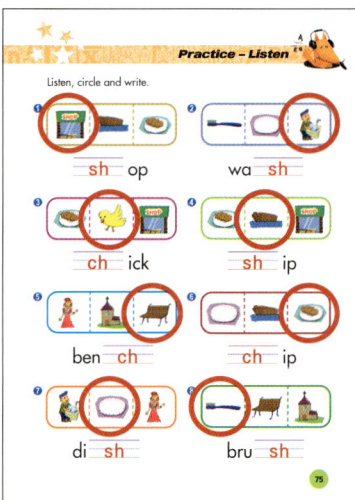

76p

❶ a
❷ a
❸ a
❹ b
❺ a
❻ a

77p

❶ sh / shape
❷ sh / brush
❸ ch / chocolate
❹ ch / rich
❺ ch / church
❻ sh / wash

78p

❶ brush
❷ ship
❸ chick
❹ wash
❺ chip
❻ shape

chick chip
chip ship shape
shape
chick
wash
brush
chick

Answer Key

82p

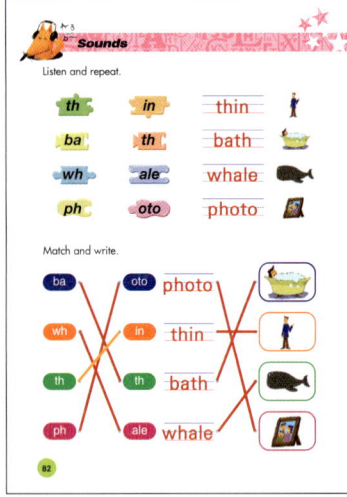

84p

85p

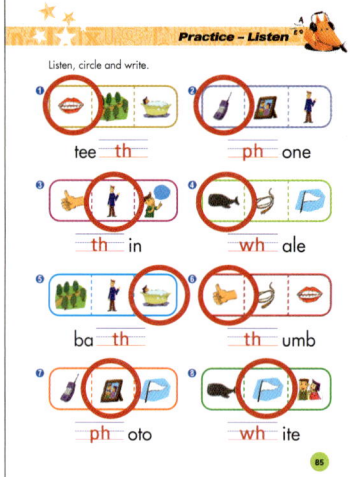

86p
❶ b
❷ a
❸ b
❹ a
❺ a
❻ b

87p
❶ wh / whisper
❷ th / path
❸ th / think
❹ wh / whip
❺ wh / whale
❻ th / thin

88p
❶ bath
❷ thumb
❸ white
❹ think
❺ whale
❻ thin

whale
whale thumb
whale
thin whisper
whale
bath
whale think

Review2

90p

① th   ② sn
③ sh   ④ ck
⑤ sw   ⑥ nk

91p

① duck   ② swim
③ white   ④ teeth
⑤ sing   ⑥ bench

92p

picture A

① 😖
② 😖
③ 🙂
④ 🙂
⑤ 🙂

93p

picture B

① 😖
② 🙂
③ 🙂
④ 🙂
⑤ 😖

Test

94, 95p

① a   ② c   ③ b
④ b   ⑤ a   ⑥ c
⑦ a   ⑧ b   ⑨ a
⑩ c   ⑪ c   ⑫ a

96, 97p

① frog / swim
② blue / stone
③ ink / dress
④ dish / sink
⑤ chick / dish
⑥ shape / ring
⑦ whisper
⑧ path

98p

① skate
② brush
③ chick
④ whale
⑤ thumb
⑥ duck

99p

❶ N

a	f	u	a	t	g
p	l	r	c	v	l
g	a	c	a	p	o
n	m	e	h	m	v
x	e	r	i	m	e
c	l	a	t	a	c

❷ F

a	b	a	n	k	e
b	e	s	a	j	d
i	n	e	c	k	y
n	c	o	r	t	i
g	h	l	e	o	m
e	d	f	a	h	p

 ANT

 BEAR

 CROCODILE

 DUCK

 ELEPHANT

 FOX

 GIRAFFE

 HARE

 IGUANA

 JELLYFISH

 KANGAROO

 LION

 MOUSE

 NIGHTINGALE

 OWL

 PIG

 QUAIL

 RACCOON

 SQUIRREL

 TIGER

 UNICORN

 VARAN

 WOLF

 X-RAY FISH

 YAK

 ZEBRA

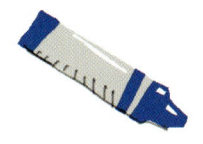

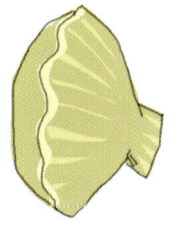

black	class	flat	brave
blue	clap	flag	brick
blade	clock	flame	bride
block	clam	flap	brass

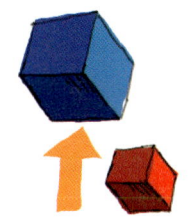

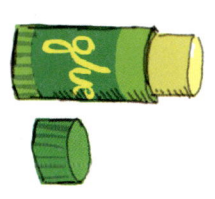

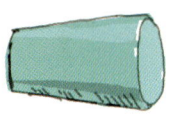

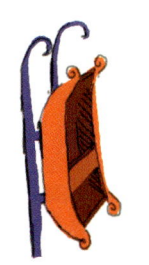

crop	frog	glass	slide
cross	frame	glove	sled
crab	front	glue	slice
craft	from	glider	slim

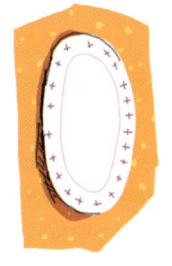
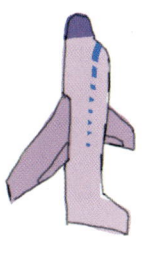

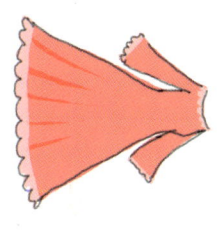

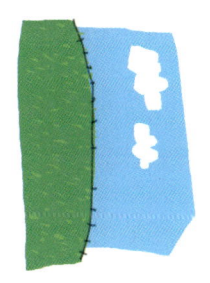

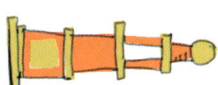

plane	dress	grass	prize
plate	drive	grape	truck
plan	drum	price	trace
plant	grab	prince	trap

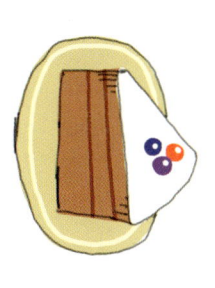

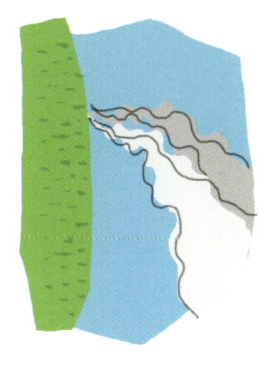

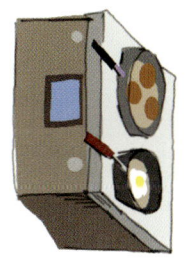

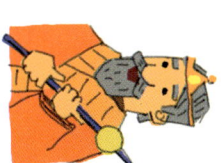

ski	snack	smell	king
skate	snake	stop	ring
swim	smile	stone	sing
sweet	smoke	stove	wing

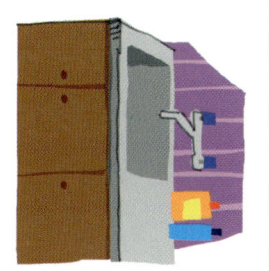
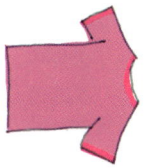

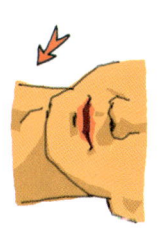

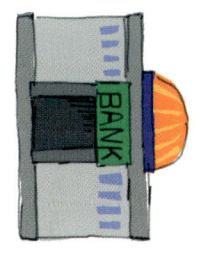

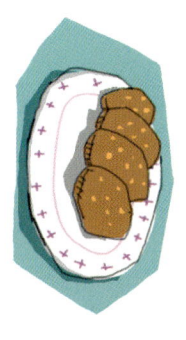

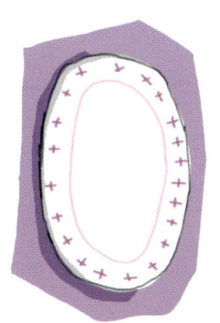

ink	bank	ship	wash
pink	sick	shop	dish
sink	neck	shape	chick
drink	duck	brush	chip

   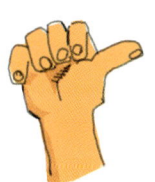

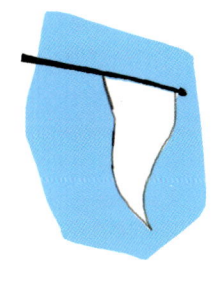 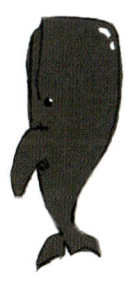  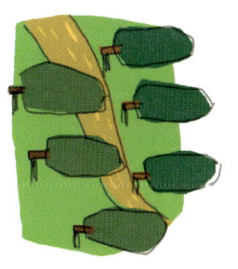

chocolate

bench

rich

church

thumb

thin

think

bath

path

teeth

whale

white

whiper

whip

photo

phone

JUMP UP

Phonics 3

개정판

Double Letter Consonants ★ Workbook

 International Linguistics Research Institute

CONTENTS

Unit 1 Double letters bl cl fl

A Check the correct picture for the beginning sounds.

B Look and Circle the correct beginning letters.

C Match the correct picture.

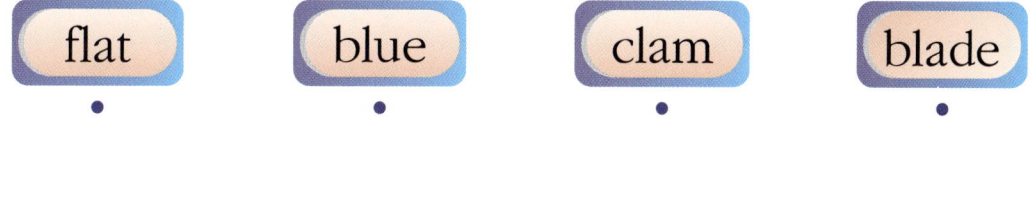

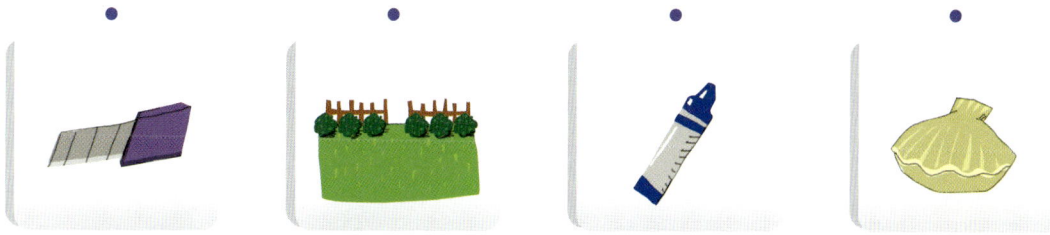

D Look and Check the correct words.

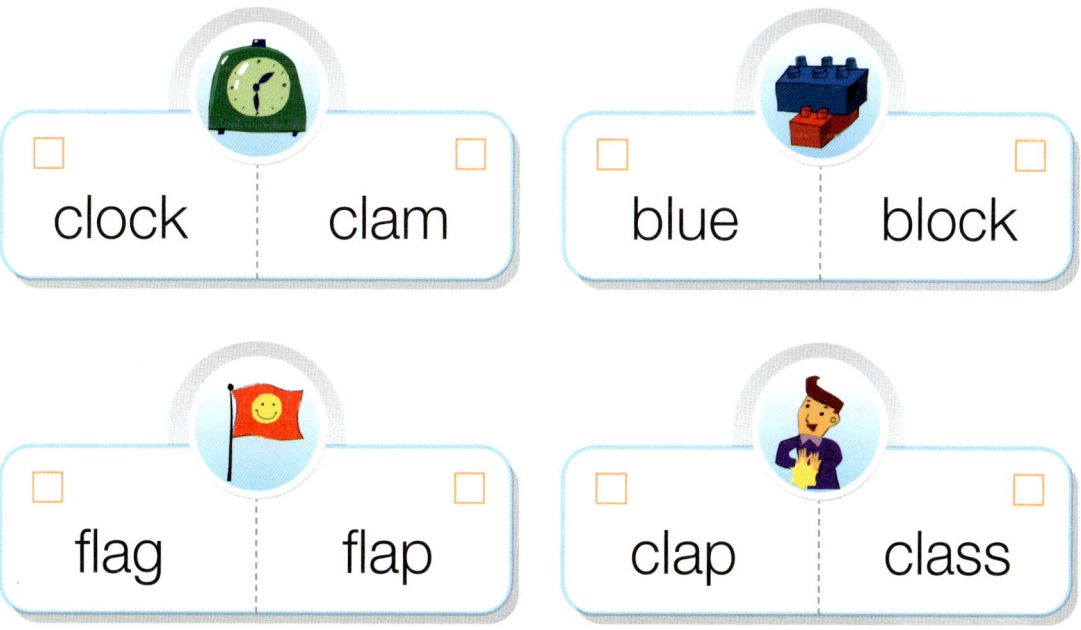

E Circle the pictures with the same beginning letters.

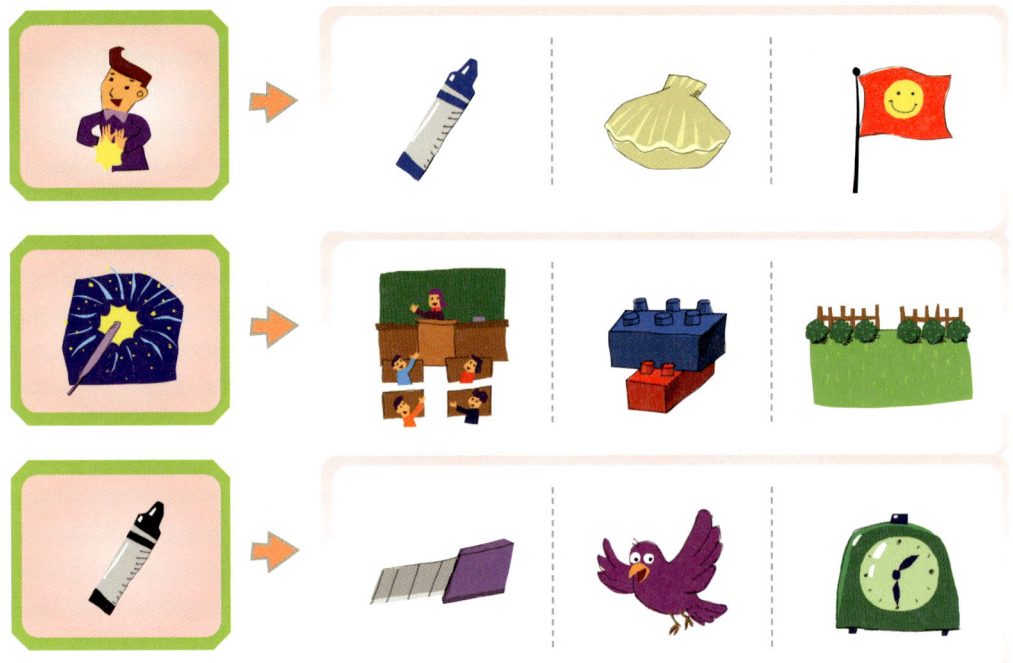

F Circle the pictures with the different beginning letters.

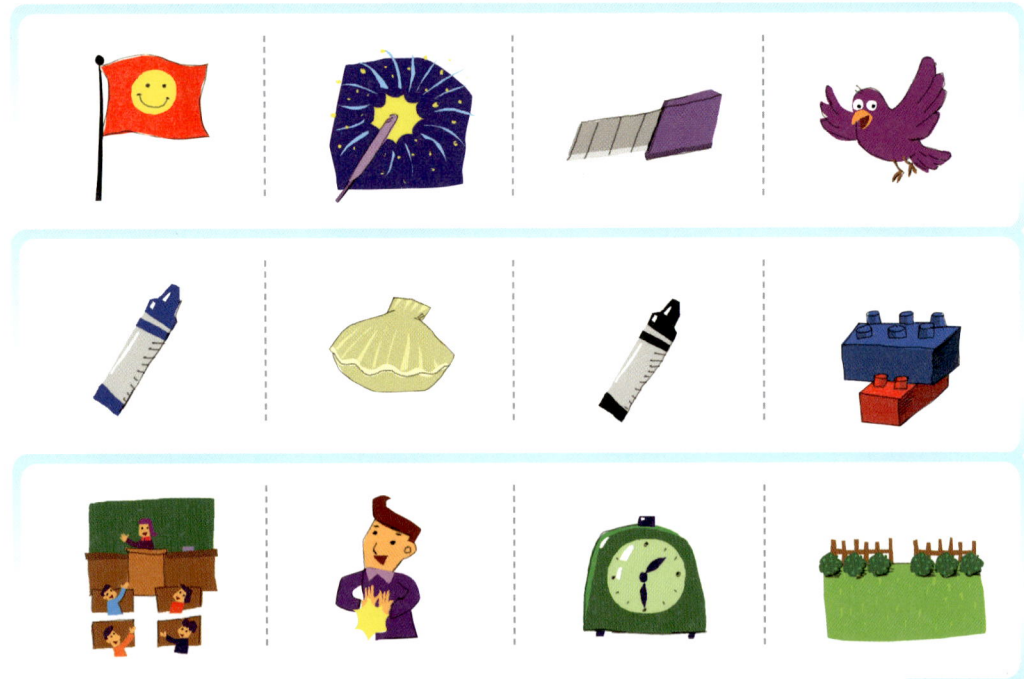

G Read and Write the blank.

The kids pile the blue _____ s.

The _____ is on the blue gate.

The men sit on the _____ mat.

The red flags _____ in the wind.

The man uses a _____ to cut the tap

There is a cute clam in the _____ .

H Look and Write.

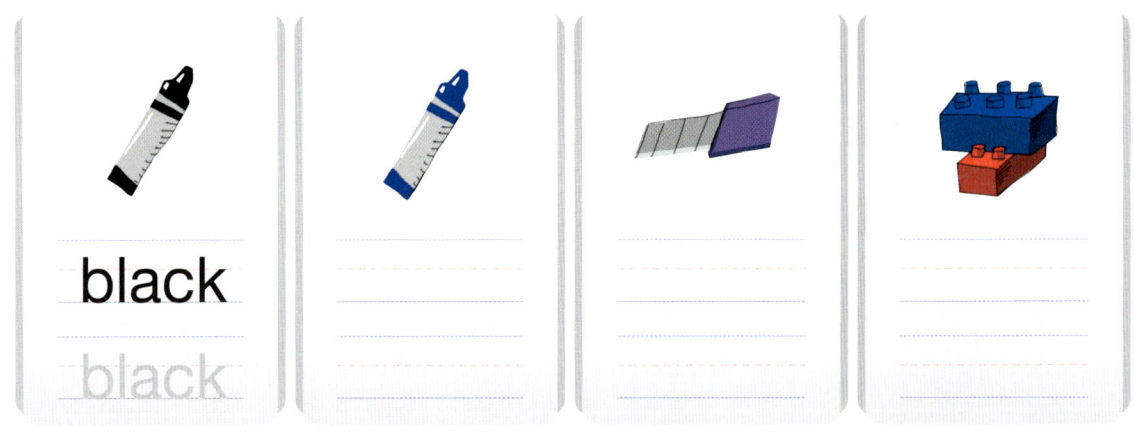

black

black

A Check the correct picture for the beginning sounds.

B Look and Circle the correct beginning letters.

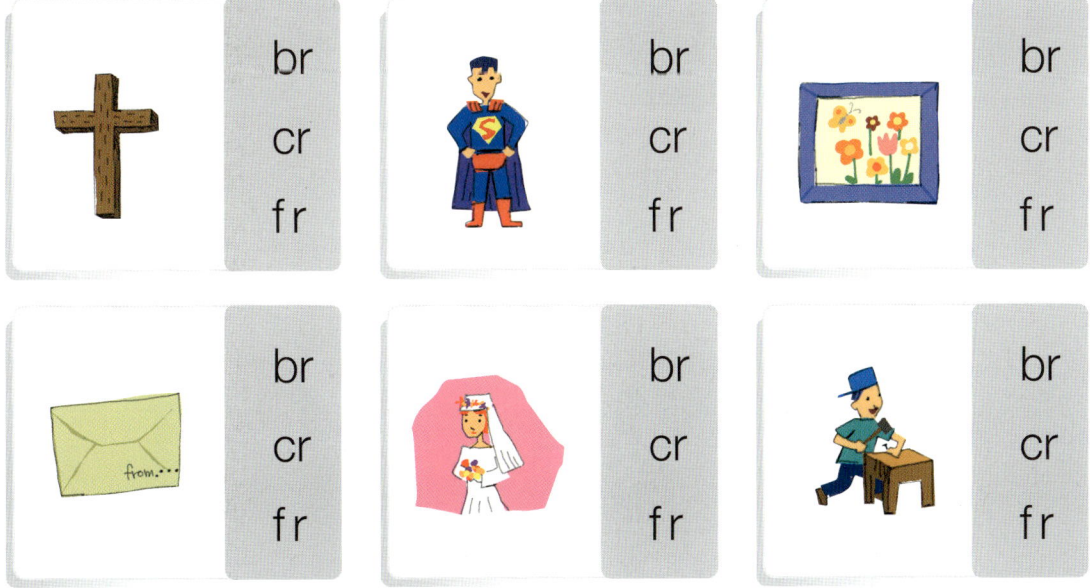

C Match the correct picture.

frog   brick   cross   front

D Look and Check the correct words.

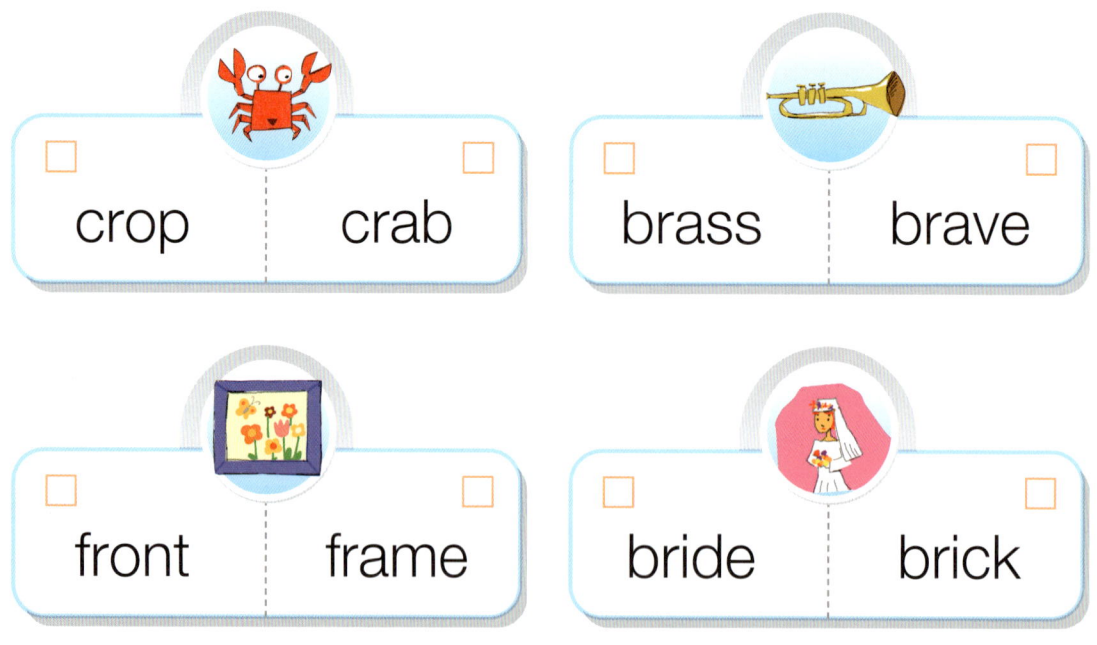

☐ crop ☐ crab

☐ brass ☐ brave

☐ front ☐ frame

☐ bride ☐ brick

E Circle the pictures with the same beginning letters.

F Circle the pictures with the different beginning letters.

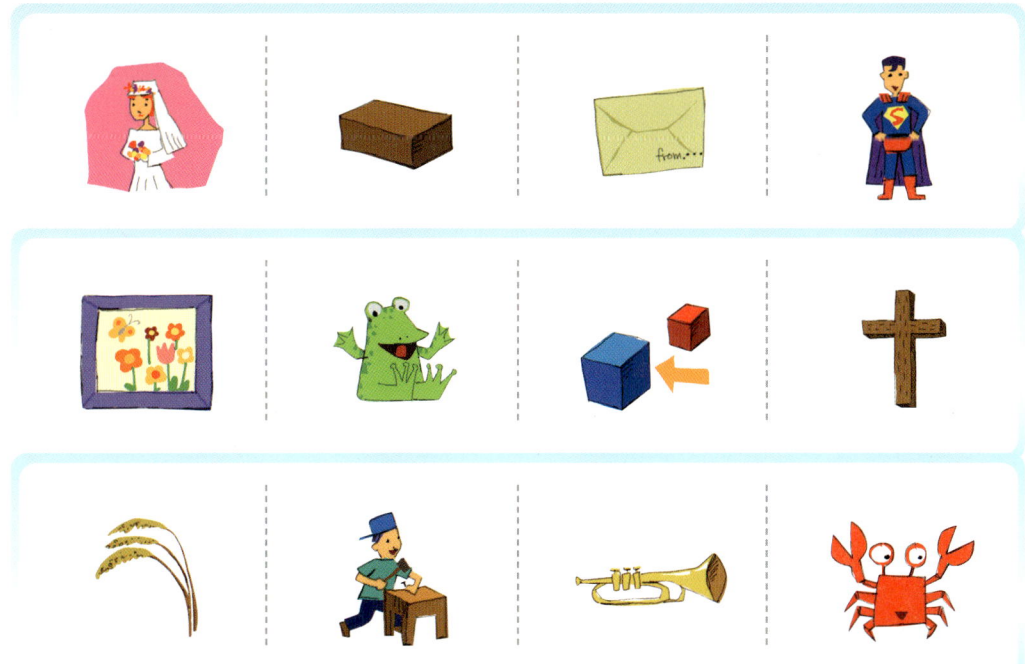

G Read and Write the blank.

 The brave _____ hit the bad man.

 The _____ is in front of the hut.

 Men play the _____ es.

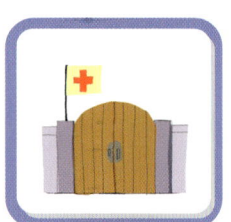 The red _____ flag is on the gate.

 The vase is on the _____ .

 The man has some _____ s.

H Look and Write.

Unit 3 Double letters gl sl pl

A Check the correct picture for the beginning sounds.

B Look and Circle the correct beginning letters.

C Match the correct picture.

plane   slide   glove   plate

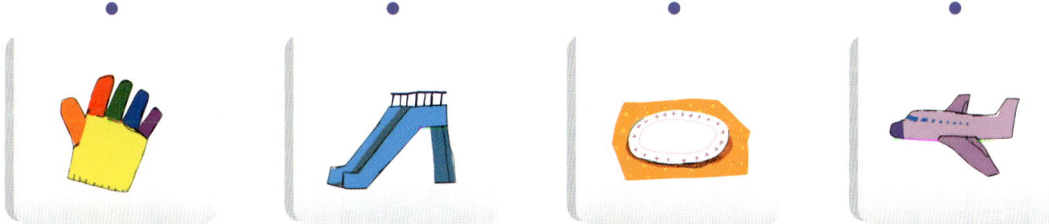

D Look and Check the correct words.

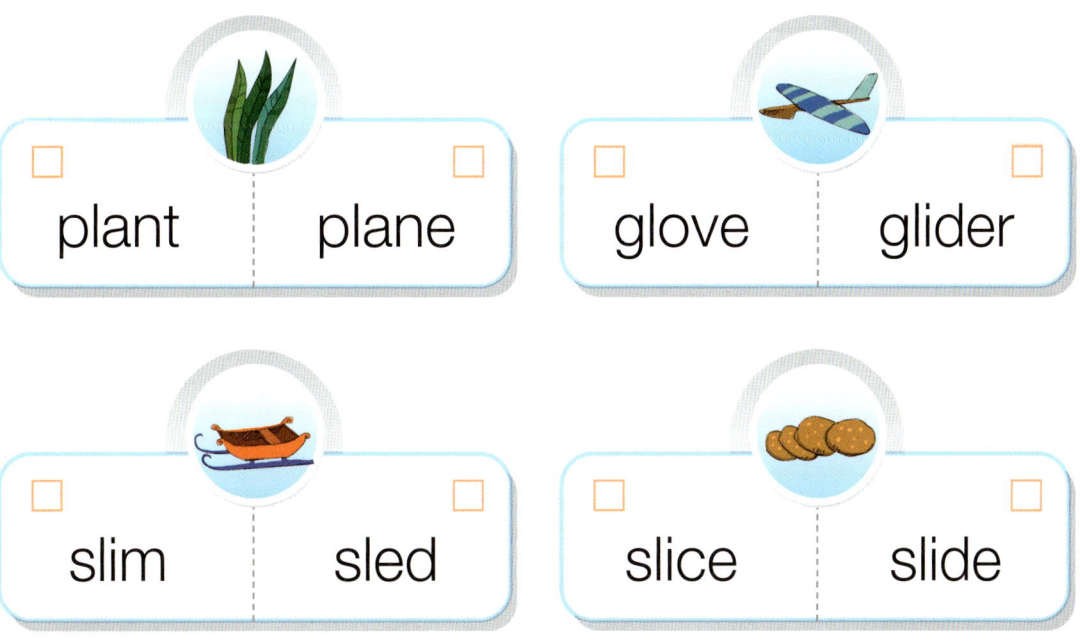

☐ plant   ☐ plane   ☐ glove   ☐ glider

☐ slim   ☐ sled   ☐ slice   ☐ slide

E Circle the pictures with the same beginning letters.

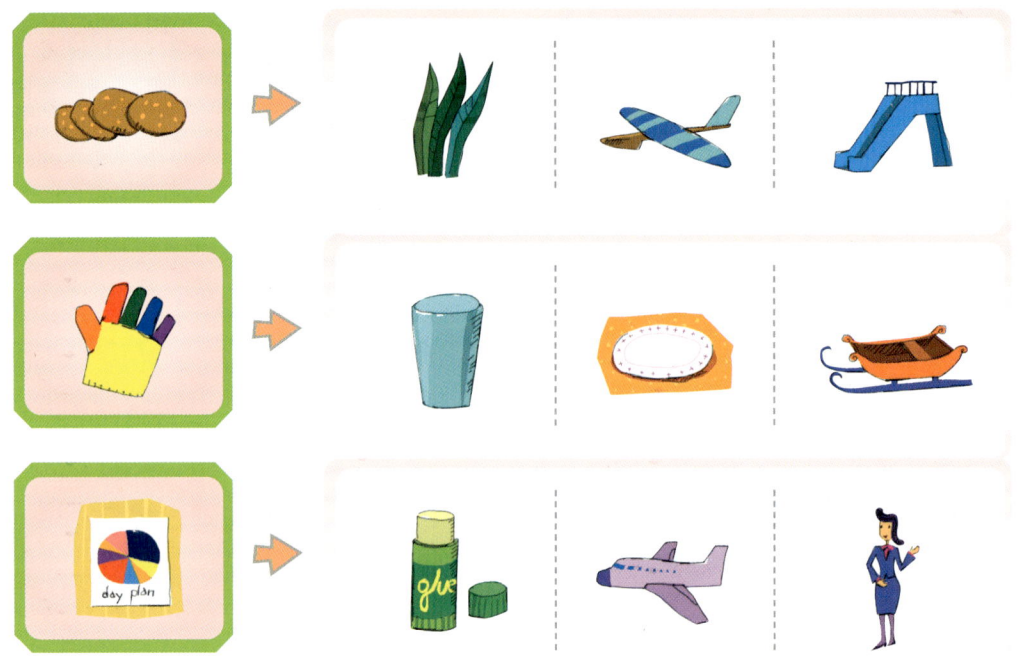

F Circle the pictures with the different beginning letters.

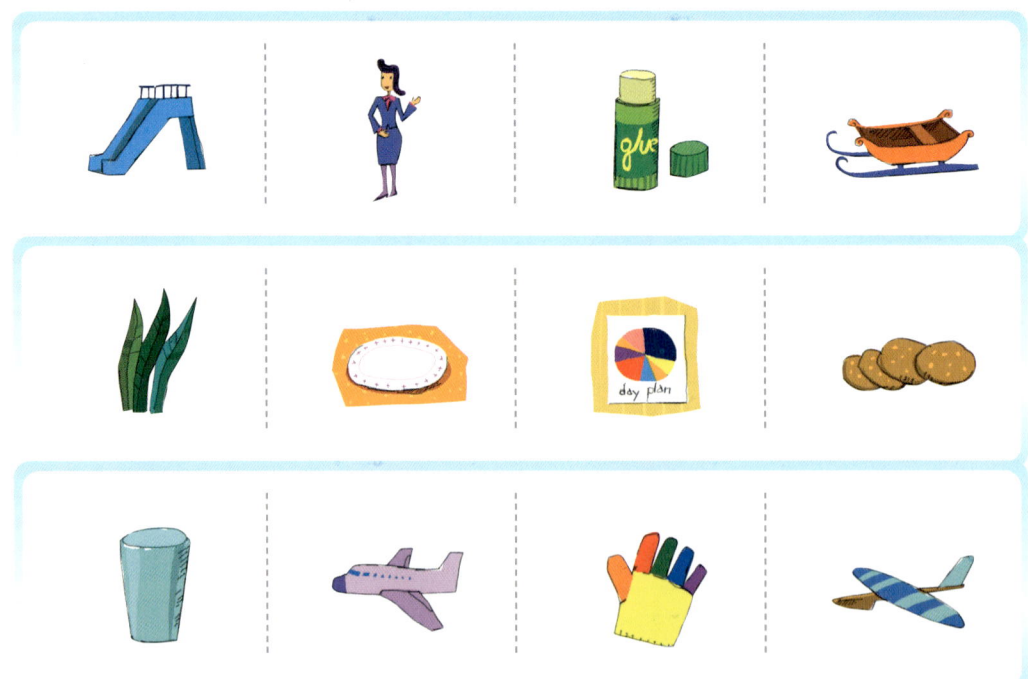

G Read and Write the blank.

The fox is _____ and the pig is fat.

Frogs ride a _____ one by one.

The cat has _____ s.

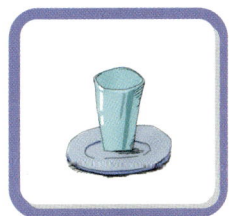

The _____ is on the plate.

The pup is in front of the _____ .

The kids sit on the _____ .

H Look and Write.

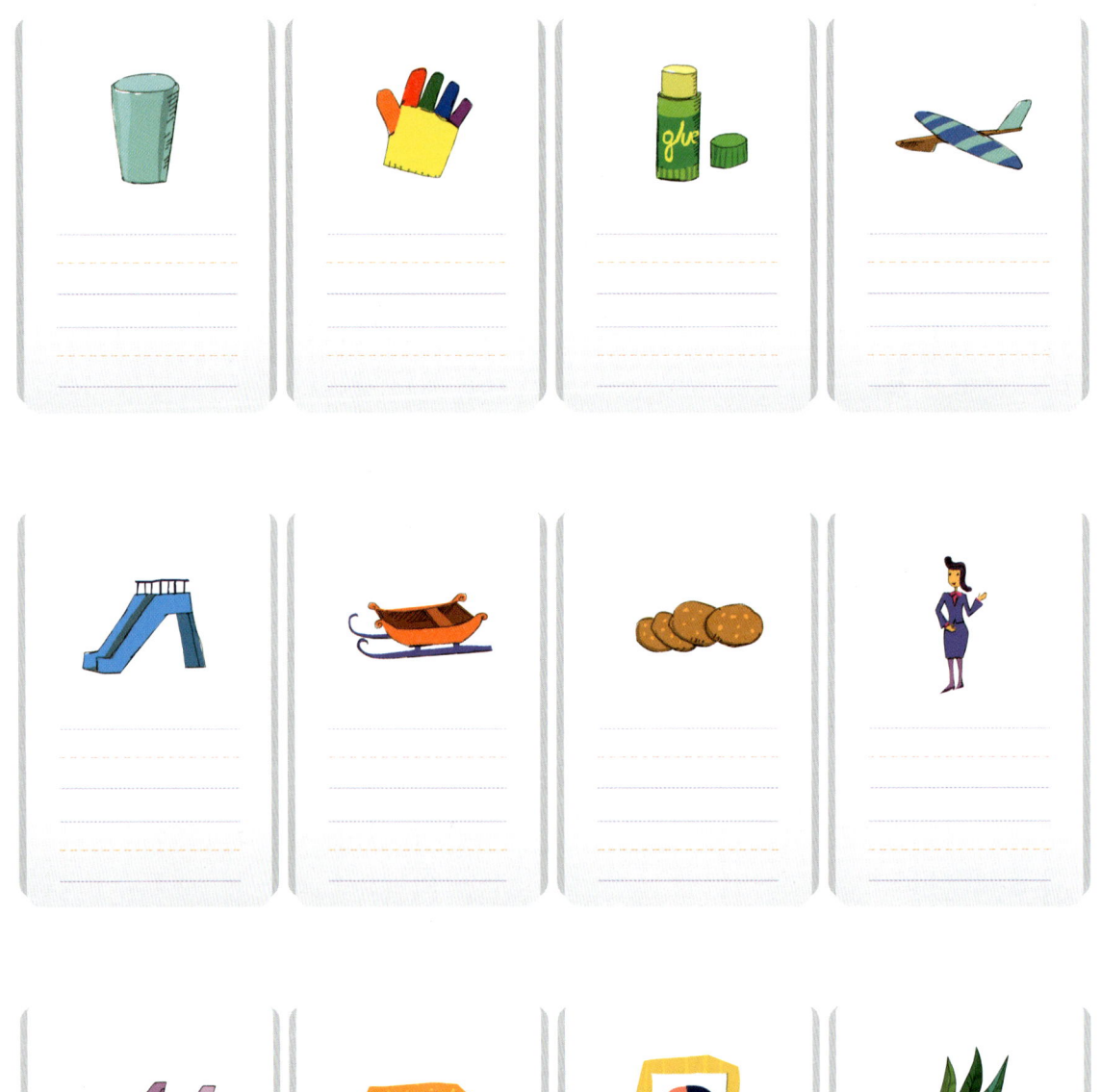

Unit 4 Double letters dr gr pr tr

A Check the correct picture for the beginning sounds.

dr ➡ ⚪ ⚪ ⚪ ⚪

gr ➡ ⚪ ⚪ ⚪ ⚪

pr ➡ ⚪ ⚪ ⚪ ⚪

tr ➡ ⚪ ⚪ ⚪ ⚪

B Look and Circle the correct beginning letters.

dr	dr	dr
gr	gr	gr
pr	pr	pr
tr	tr	tr

C Match the correct picture.

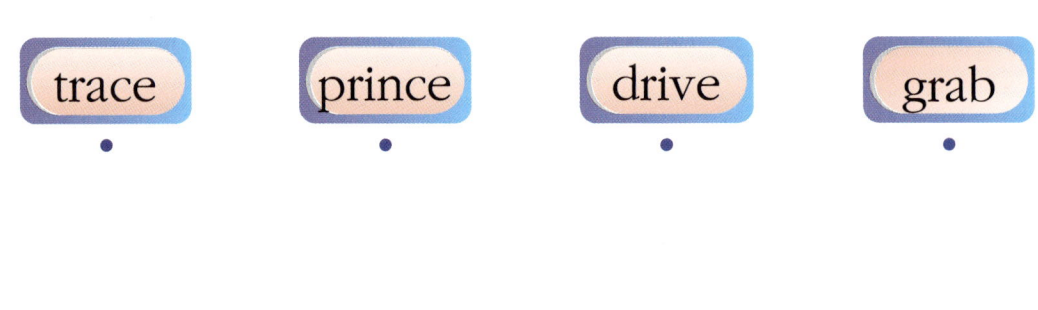

D Look and Check the correct words.

E Circle the pictures with the same beginning letters.

F Circle the pictures with the different beginning letters.

Read and Write the blank.

The kids get the _____.

There is a _____ in front of the pine.

The bride has _____ in the pot.

The prince plays the _____.

The crab _____ s the slices of ham.

Dad _____ s the glass.

H Look and Write.

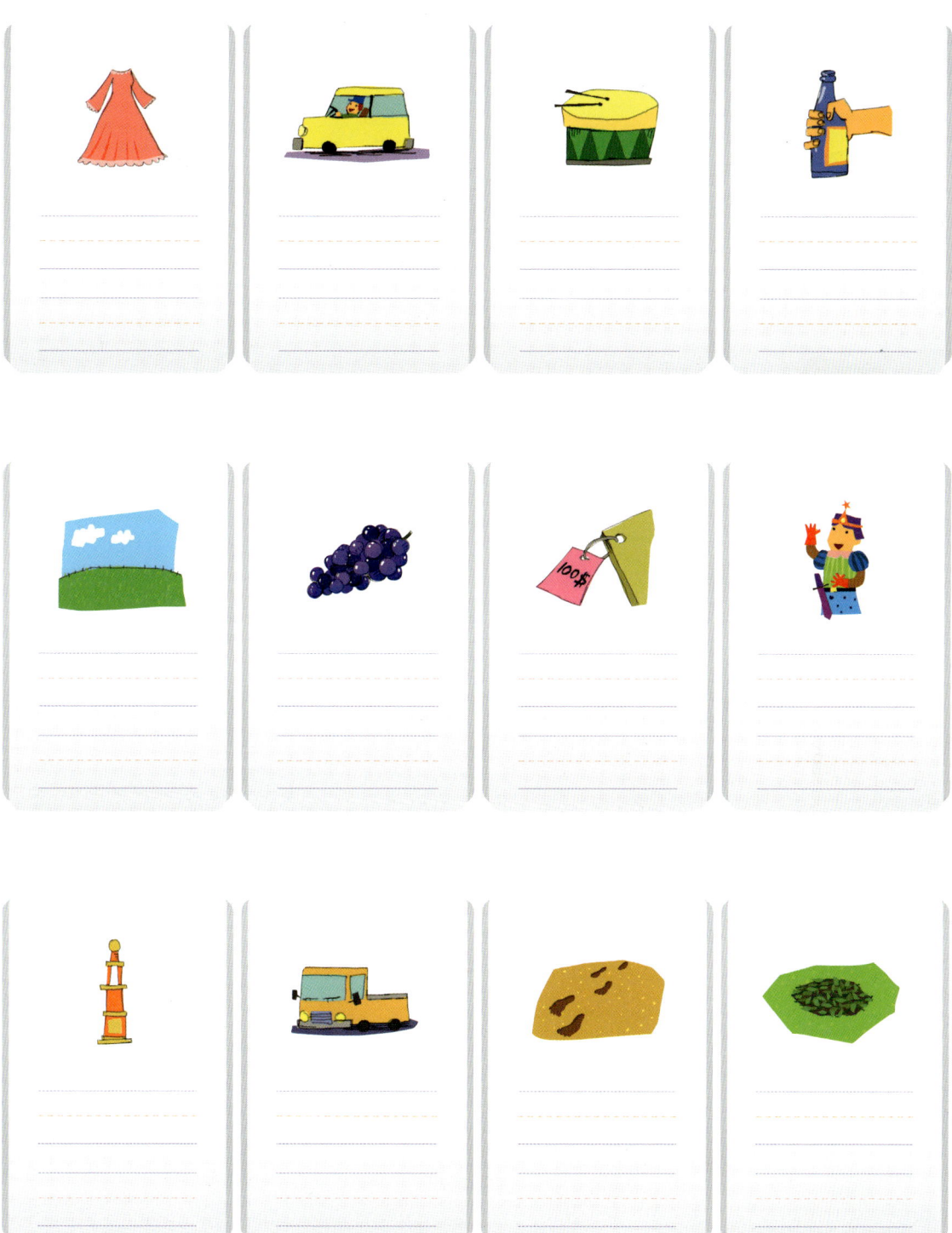

A Check the right word for the picture.

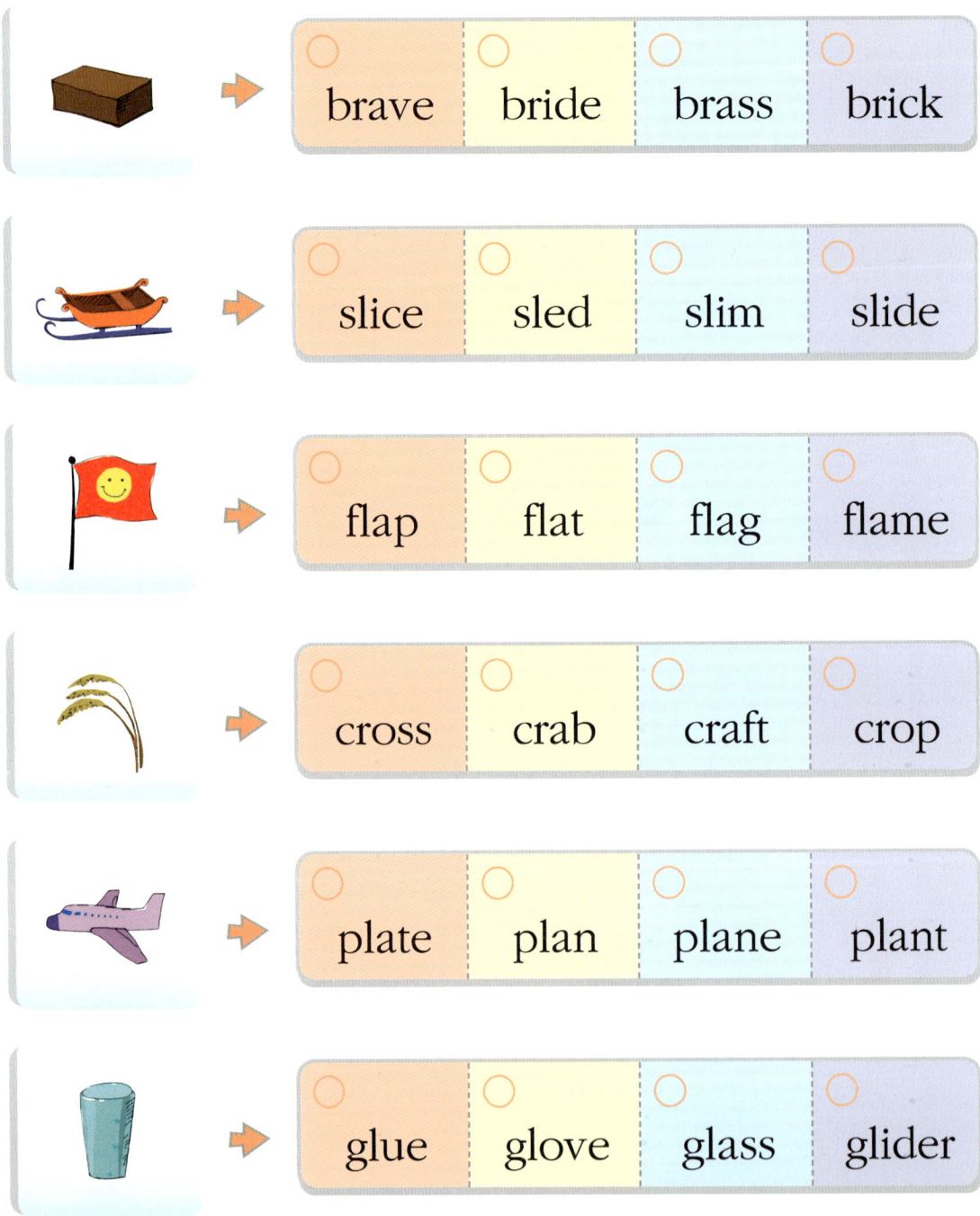

🔘	brave	○ bride	○ brass	○ brick
○	slice	○ sled	○ slim	○ slide
○	flap	○ flat	○ flag	○ flame
○	cross	○ crab	○ craft	○ crop
○	plate	○ plan	○ plane	○ plant
○	glue	○ glove	○ glass	○ glider

B Look and Match.

 • •  • •

 • •  • •

 • •  • •

 • •  • •

 • •  • •

 • •  • •

•  • •

C Choose and Write correct letters.

tr fr sl gl bl cr fl br pr cl dr pl

1. ⬜ ⬜ i d e
2. ⬜ ⬜ e s s
3. ⬜ ⬜ a n
4. ⬜ ⬜ a c e
5. ⬜ ⬜ o m
6. ⬜ ⬜ u e
7. ⬜ ⬜ a t
8. ⬜ ⬜ i z e
9. ⬜ ⬜ a m
10. ⬜ ⬜ a f t
11. ⬜ ⬜ a s s
12. ⬜ ⬜ o v e

D Check the right letters.

☐ pl ☐ fl ☐ pr ☐ fr

☐ cr ☐ cl ☐ fl ☐ fr

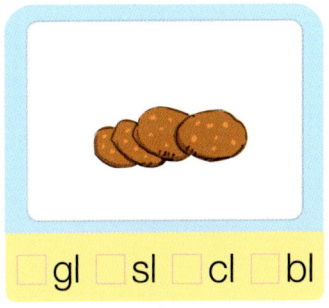

☐ gl ☐ sl ☐ cl ☐ bl

☐ pl ☐ fl ☐ pr ☐ fr

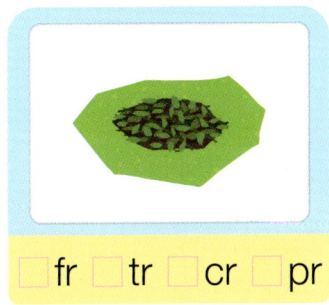

☐ fr ☐ tr ☐ cr ☐ pr

☐ dr ☐ cr ☐ tr ☐ gr

E Match the right picture.

 truck

 plate

 block

 prince

Write the missing letters.

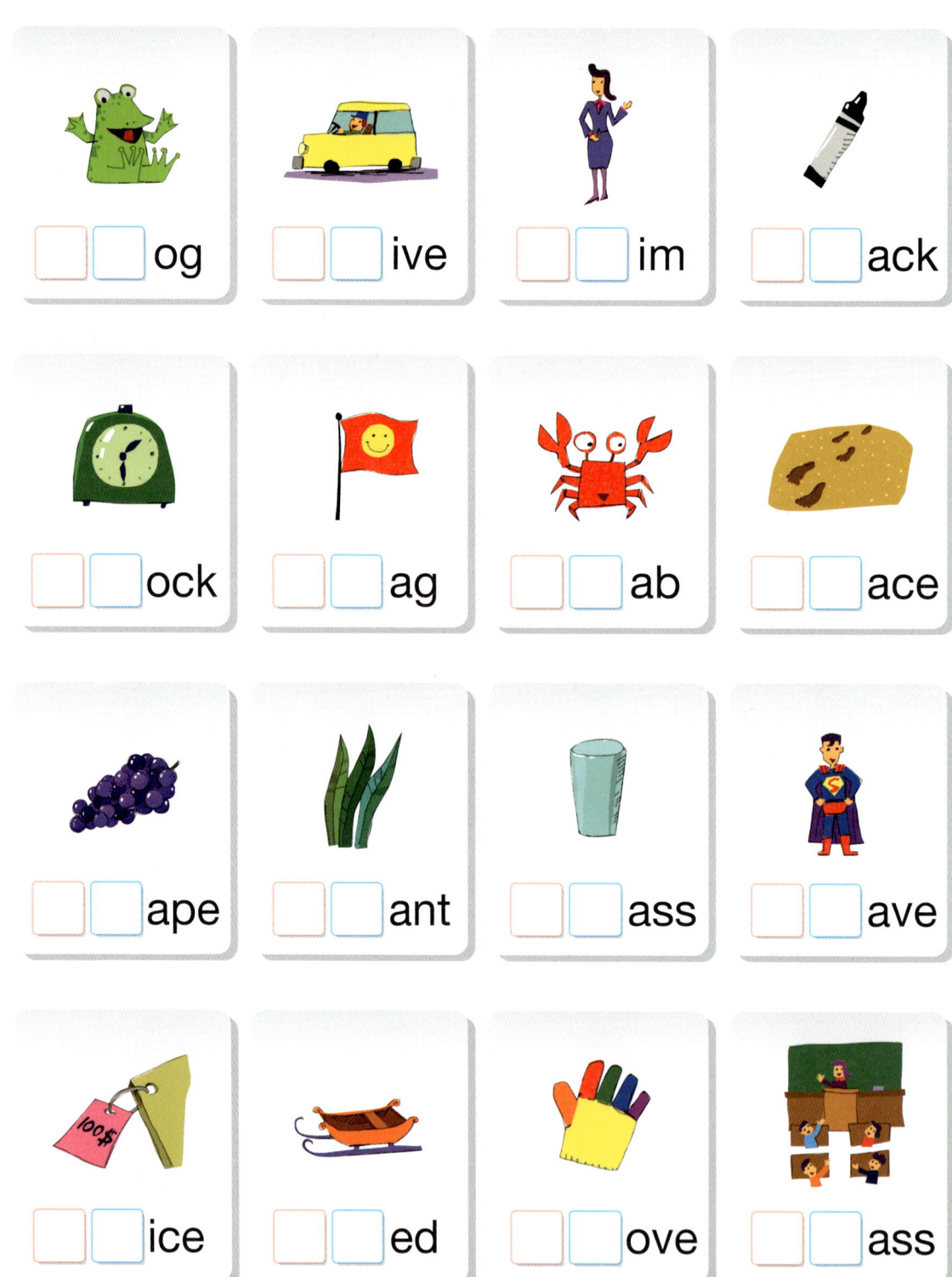

___og

___ive

___im

___ack

___ock

___ag

___ab

___ace

___ape

___ant

___ass

___ave

___ice

___ed

___ove

___ass

Unit 5 Double letters sk sm sn st sw

A Check the correct picture for the beginning sounds.

sk

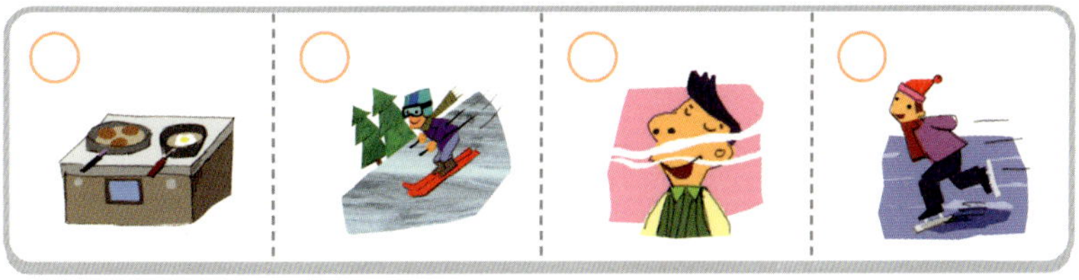

sw

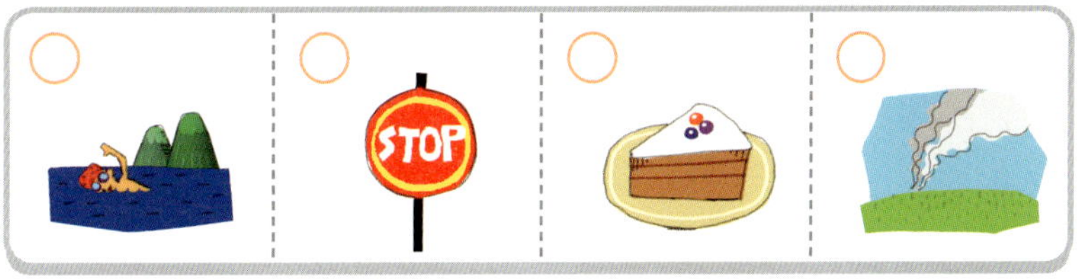

sn

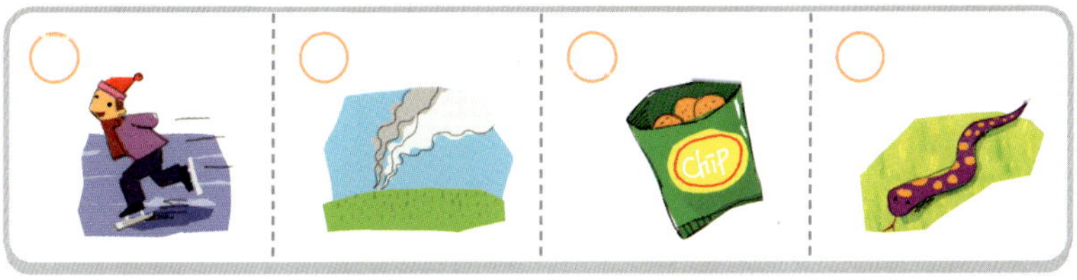

sm

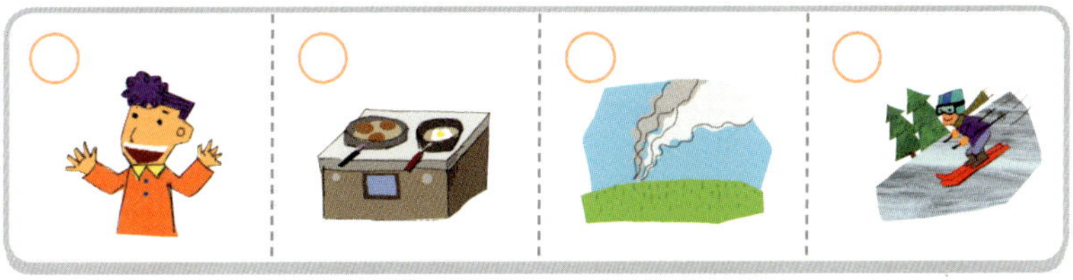

st

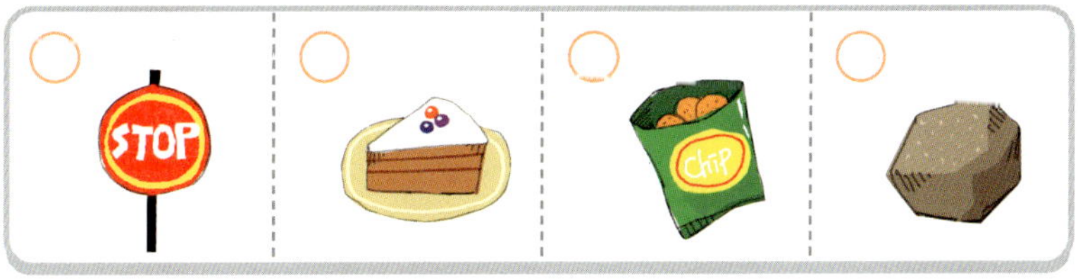

B Look and Circle the correct beginning letters.

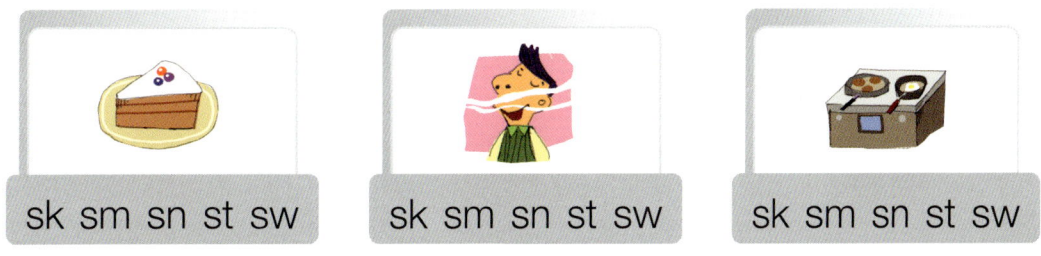

sk sm sn st sw

sk sm sn st sw

sk sm sn st sw

C Match the correct picture.

smell   stove   ski   snack

D Look and Check the correct words.

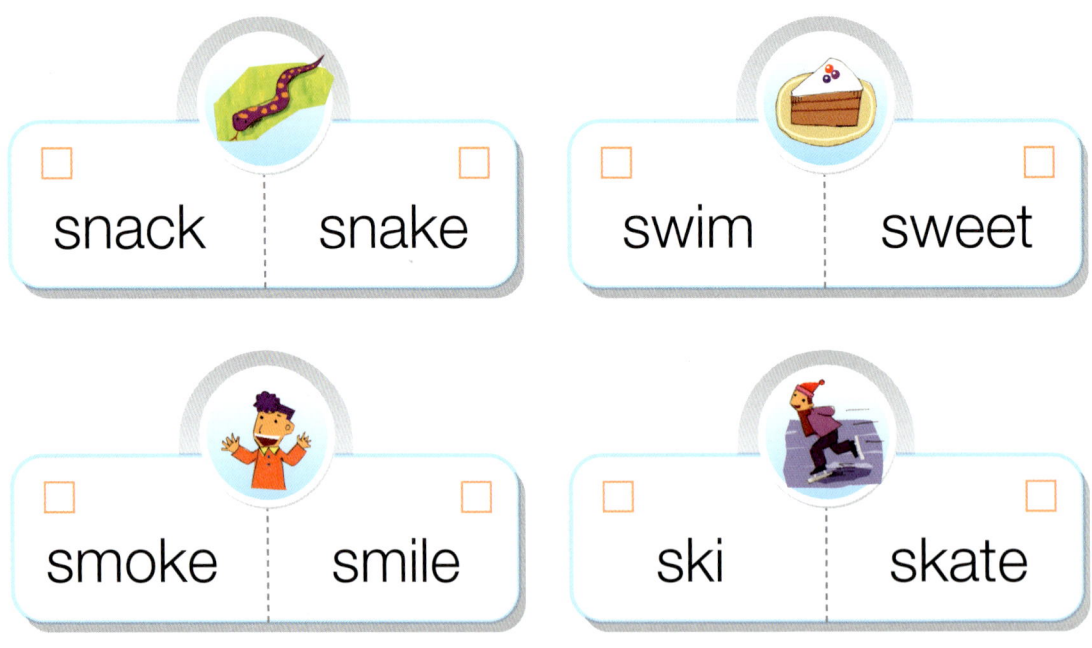

☐ snack   ☐ snake

☐ swim   ☐ sweet

☐ smoke   ☐ smile

☐ ski   ☐ skate

E Circle the pictures with the same beginning letters.

F Circle the pictures with the different beginning letters.

G Read and Write the blank.

The blue pot is on the _____.

The _____ is on the grass.

The bride _____s at the rose.

The men _____ on the ice.

The frog _____s in the lake.

The snacks are on the _____.

H Look and Write.

Unit 6 Double letters ng nk ck

A Check the correct picture for the ending sounds.

B Look and Circle the correct ending letters.

C Match the correct picture.

sick	sing	sink	neck

D Look and Check the correct words.

☐ ring ☐ wing

☐ duck ☐ neck

☐ ink ☐ pink

☐ king ☐ sing

E Circle the pictures with the same ending letters.

F Circle the pictures with the different ending letters.

Ⓖ Read and Write the blank.

The duck has a _____ ring

The plates are in the _____.

The ducks _____ with a hose.

The _____ is on the dress.

The kid _____ s with a duck.

The _____ has a blue wing.

Look and Write.

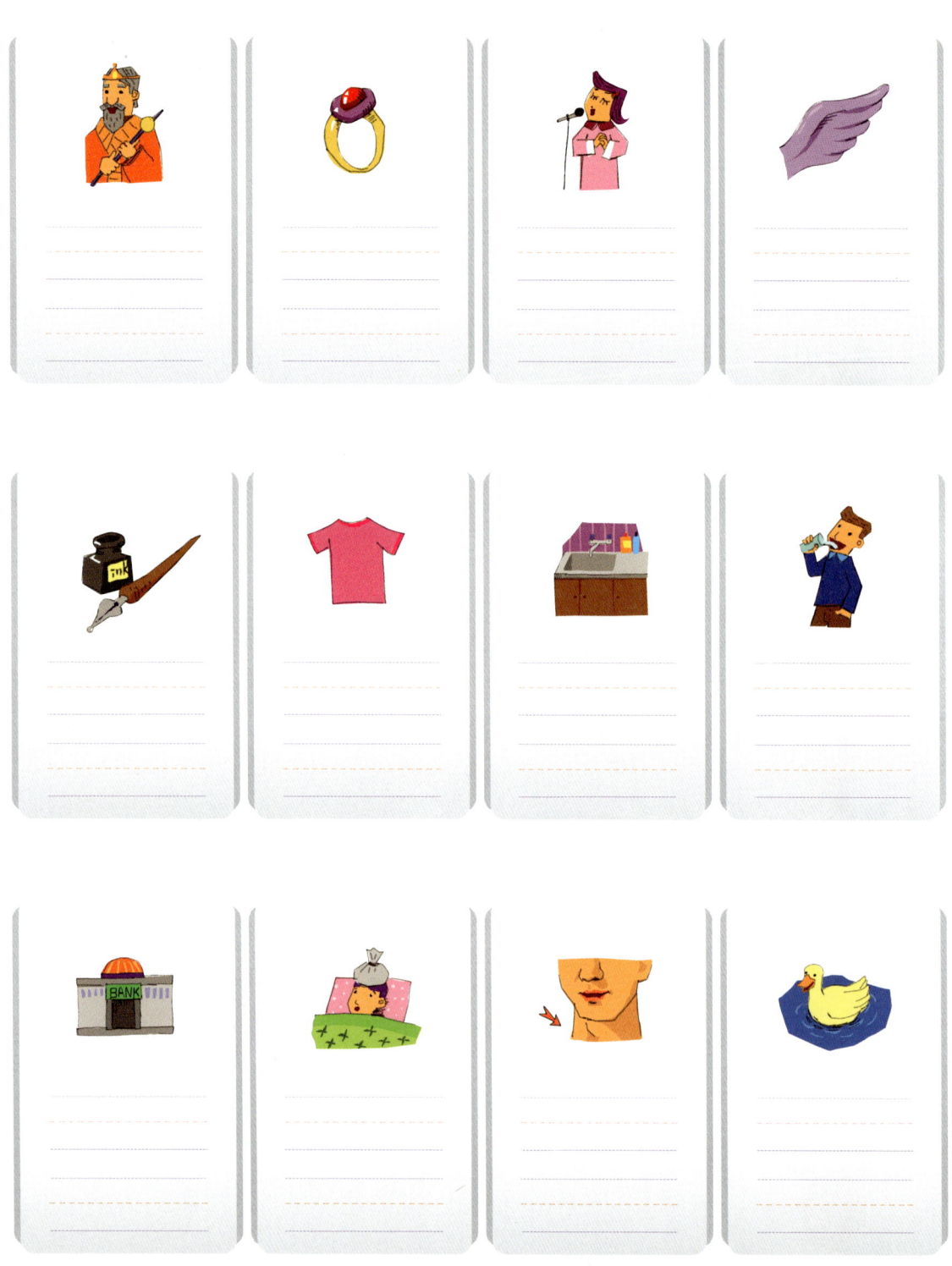

Unit 7 Double letters sh ch

A Check the correct picture for the same letters.

sh~ ➡ ○ ○ ○ ○

~sh ➡ ○ ○ ○ ○

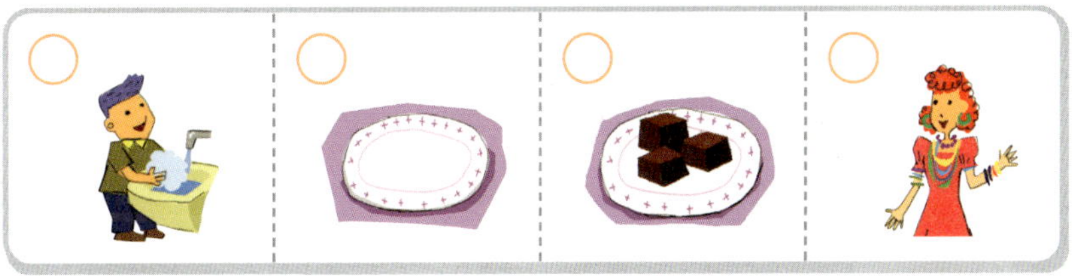

ch~ ➡ ○ ○ ○ ○

~ch ➡ ○ ○ ○ ○

B Look and Circle the correct same letters.

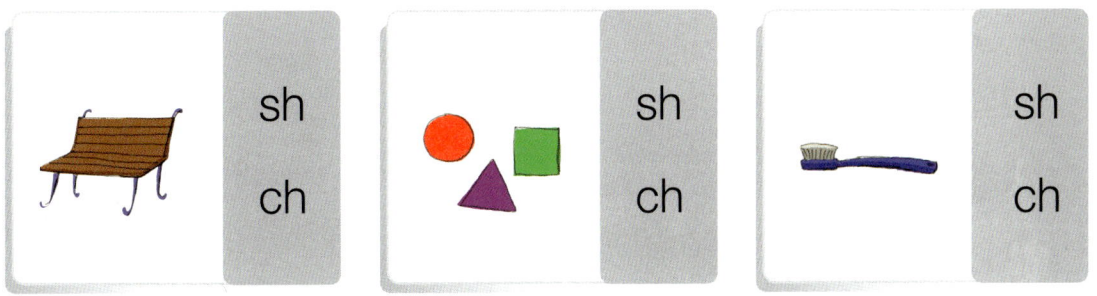

sh
ch

sh
ch

sh
ch

C Match the correct picture.

shop	wash	chip	rich

D Look and Check the correct words.

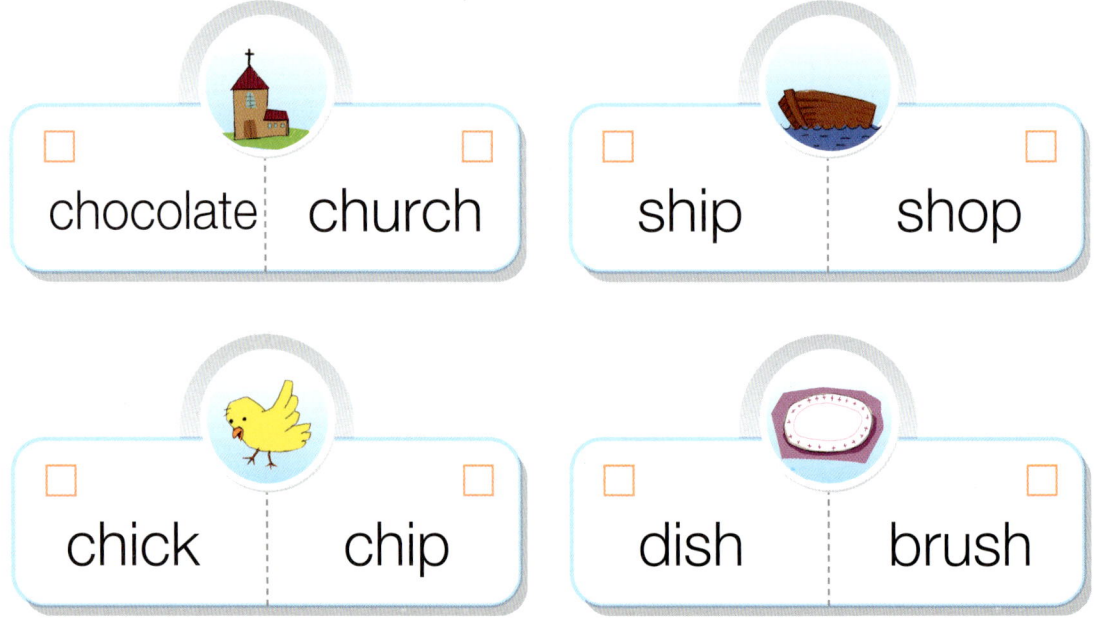

☐ chocolate	☐ church

☐ ship	☐ shop

☐ chick	☐ chip

☐ dish	☐ brush

E Circle the pictures with the same beginning / ending letters.

F Circle the pictures with the different beginning / ending letters.

G Read and Write the blank.

 The chicks wash the _____.

 The kid has _____s.

 The rich king has a big _____.

 The _____ is on the bench.

 The bench is in front of the _____.

 The _____ of the chip is a ring.

H Look and Write.

Unit 8 Double letters th wh ph

A Check the correct picture for the same letters.

th~ ➡ ⭕ ⭕ ⭕ ⭕

~th ➡ ⭕ ⭕ ⭕ ⭕

wh~ ➡ ⭕ ⭕ ⭕ ⭕

ph~ ➡ ⭕ ⭕ ⭕ ⭕

B Look and Circle the correct beginning letters.

| | th wh ph | | th wh ph | | th wh ph |

C Match the correct picture.

  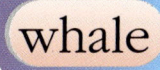 

thumb · teeth · whale · whip ·

D Look and Check the correct words.

☐ think ☐ thin

☐ whip ☐ whisper

☐ bath ☐ path

☐ photo ☐ phone

E Circle the pictures with the same beginning letters.

F Circle the pictures with the different beginning/ending letters.

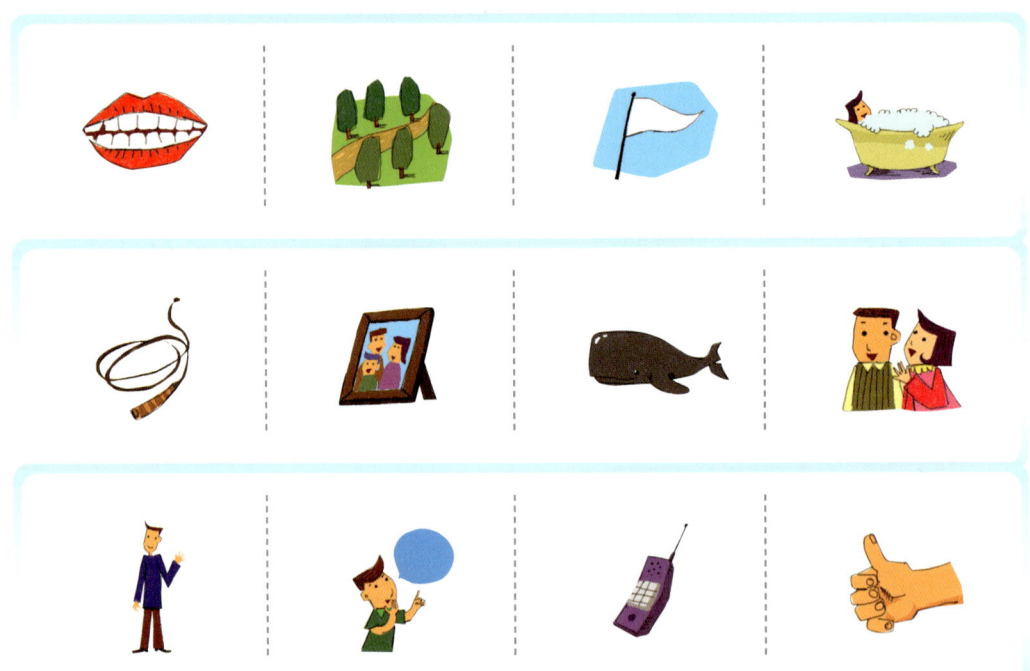

G Read and Write the blank.

The _____ has white teeth.

The _____ man takes a bath.

The man is on the _____ .

The kids _____ to mom.

The kid hurts his _____ .

The chick has the _____ .

H Look and Write.

A Check the right word for the picture.

	sing	wing	ring	king
○	○	○	○	

	snake	snack	smile	smoke

	ink	sink	bank	pink

	bath	path	thin	thumb

	dish	wash	ship	shop

	whale	whisper	whip	white

B Look and Match.

 ph •

 •

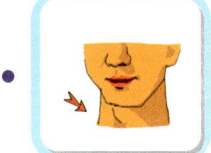 •

 sw •

 •

 •

 ck •

 •

 •

 st •

 •

 •

 sm •

 •

 •

 wh •

 •

 •

ch •

 •

 •

C Choose and Write correct letters.

| sm | th | ck | sk | ng | ch | th | sh | nk | wh | sn | sh |

1 t e e ☐ ☐

2 b e n ☐ ☐

3 ☐ ☐ i p

4 r i ☐ ☐

5 p i ☐ ☐

6 ☐ ☐ a t e

7 ☐ ☐ i s p e r

8 s i ☐ ☐

9 ☐ ☐ a k e

10 ☐ ☐ i n k

11 d i ☐ ☐

12 ☐ ☐ o k e

D Check the right letters.

☐ ch ☐ sh ☐ th ☐ wh

☐ nk ☐ ck ☐ ng ☐ ph

☐ th ☐ ph ☐ ch ☐ sh

☐ ck ☐ ch ☐ sh ☐ th

☐ nk ☐ ng ☐ ck ☐ th

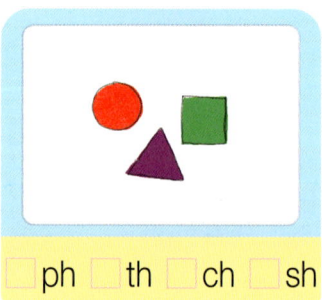

☐ ph ☐ th ☐ ch ☐ sh

E Match the right picture.

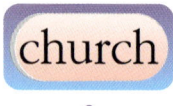 church

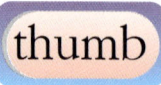 thumb

 ink

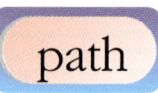 path

F Write the missing letters.

 ki☐☐

 ☐☐i

 ☐☐ove

 ☐☐oto

 si☐☐

 ☐☐ip

 pa☐☐

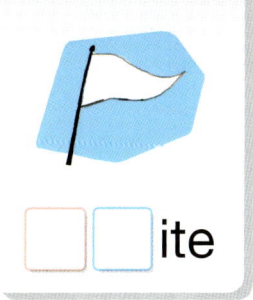 ☐☐ite

 wa☐☐

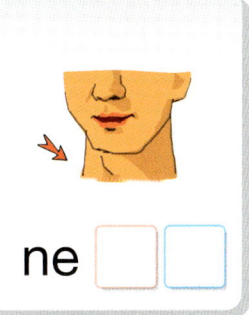 ne☐☐

 ☐☐ick

 ben☐☐

 ☐☐in

 ☐☐ile

 ☐☐im

 ☐☐op

Final Test

A Look and Match the same beginning letters.

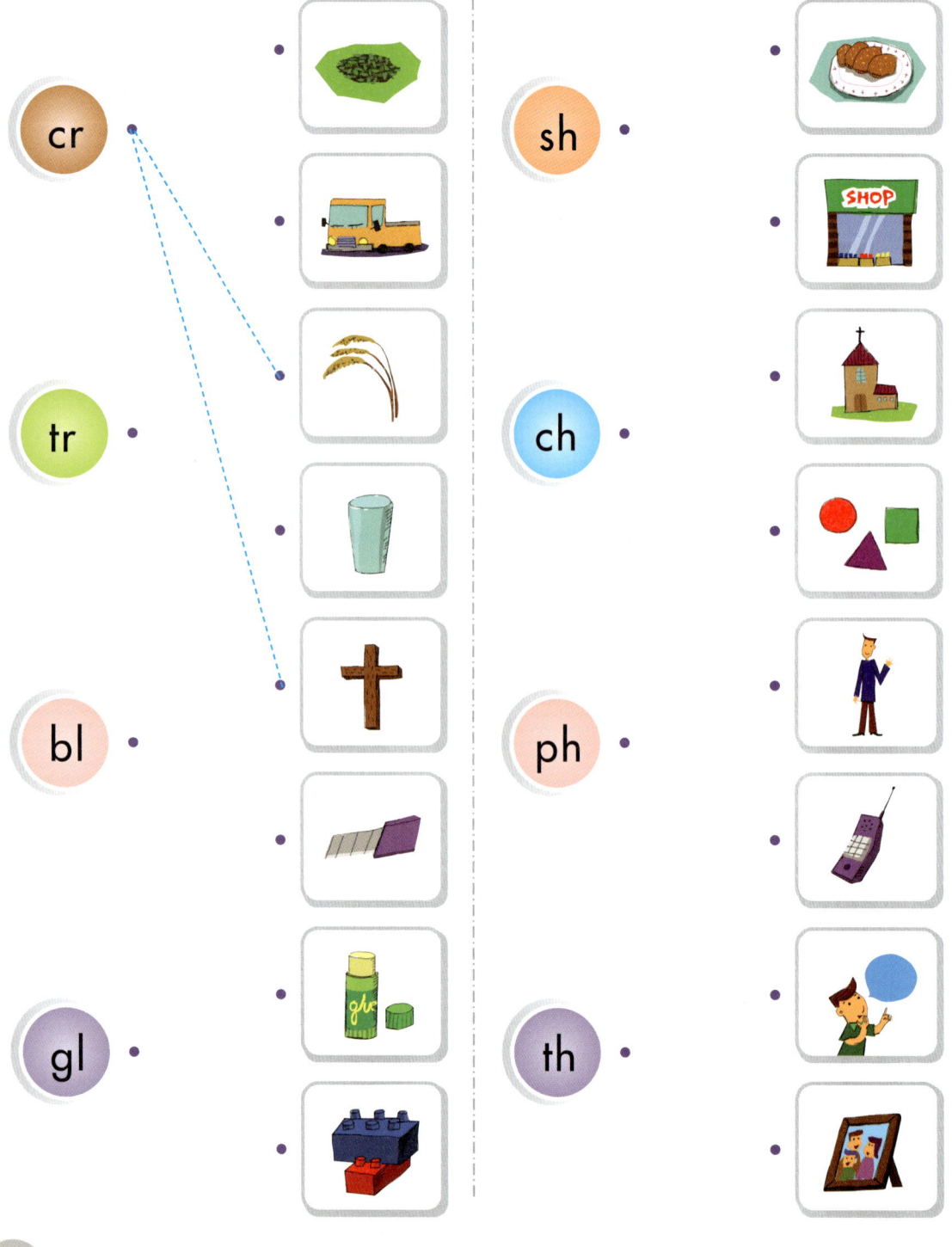

B Write the ending letters.

ri _____

ben _____

tee _____

pi _____

di _____

wi _____

du _____

ri _____

dri _____

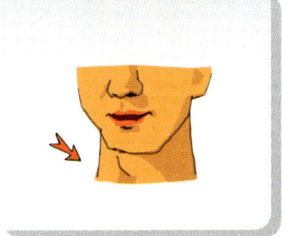

ne _____

wa _____

ba _____

Circle the correct pictures.

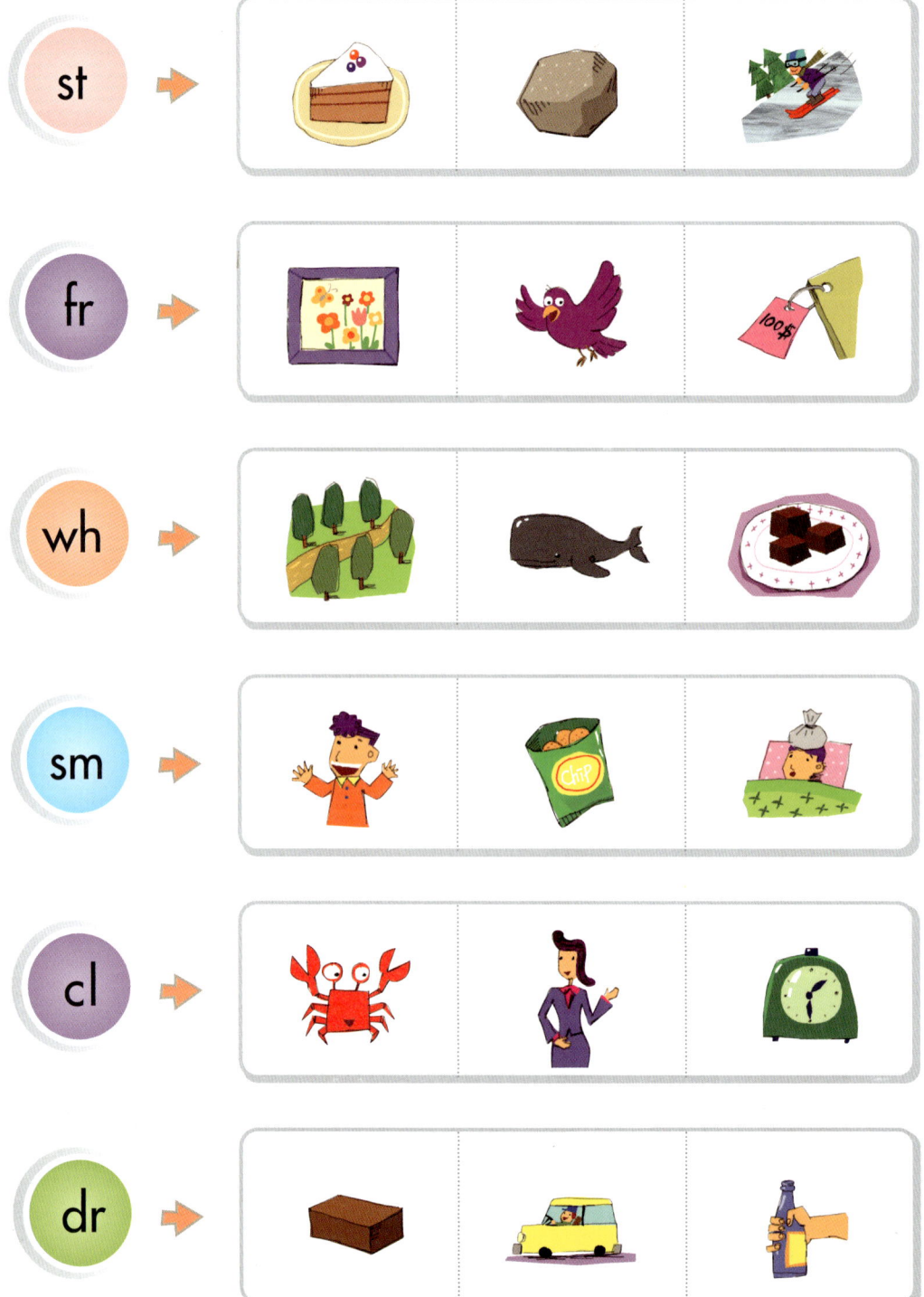

st

fr

wh

sm

cl

dr

D Do the puzzle.

Write the correct words.

_____ _____ _____ _____

_____ _____ _____ _____

_____ _____ _____ _____

   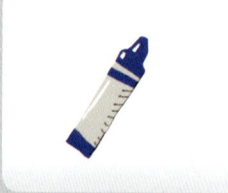

_____ _____ _____ _____

124p

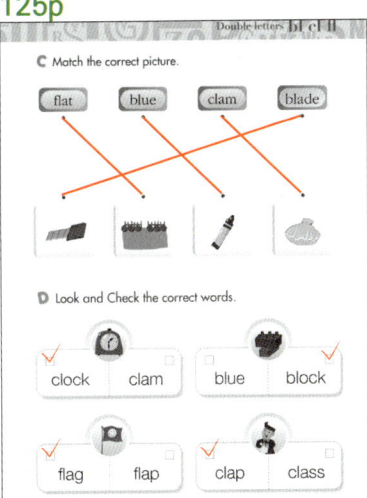
125p

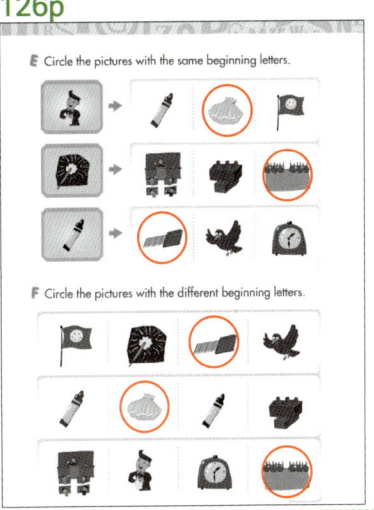
126p

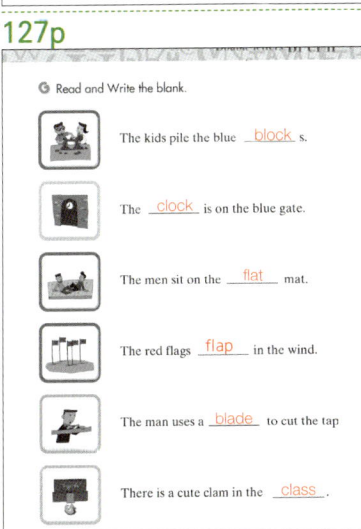
127p

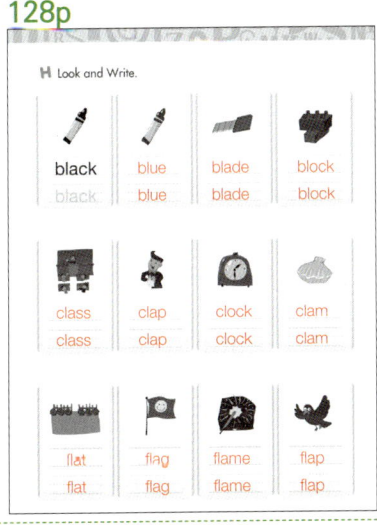
128p

129p

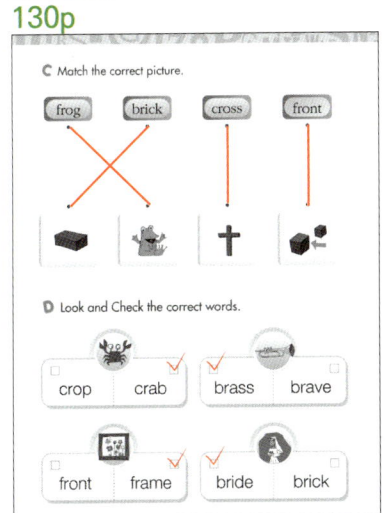
130p

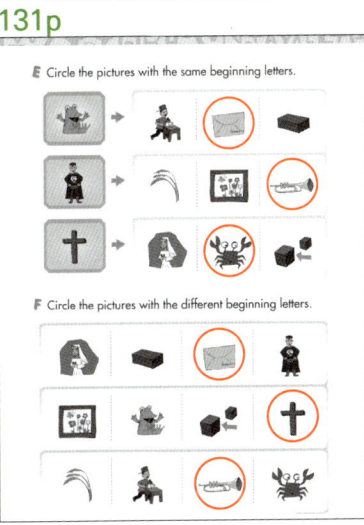
131p

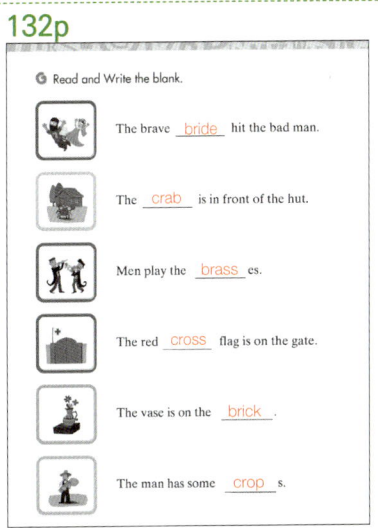
132p

Answer Key

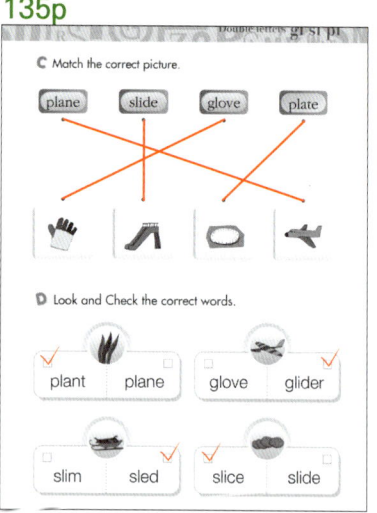

133p

H Look and Write.

brave	brick	bride	brass
brave	brick	bride	brass

crop	cross	crab	craft
crop	cross	crab	craft

frog	frame	front	from
frog	frame	front	from

134p

Unit 3 Double letters gl sl pl

A Check the correct picture for the beginning sounds.

gl →
sl →
pl →

B Look and Circle the correct beginning letters.

gl sl pl

135p

Double letters gl sl pl

C Match the correct picture.

plane slide glove plate

D Look and Check the correct words.

| plant | plane | glove | glider |
| slim | sled | slice | slide |

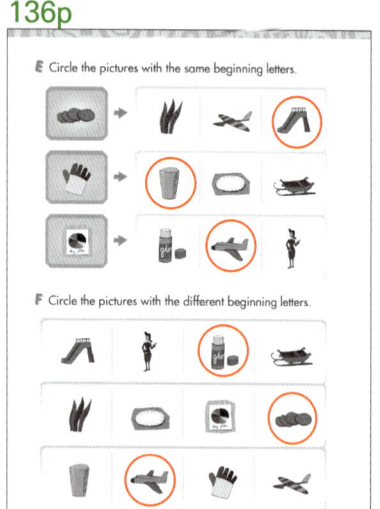
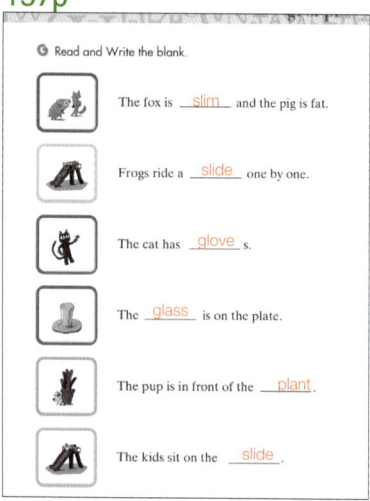

136p

E Circle the pictures with the same beginning letters.

F Circle the pictures with the different beginning letters.

137p

G Read and Write the blank.

The fox is ___slim___ and the pig is fat.

Frogs ride a ___slide___ one by one.

The cat has ___glove___ s.

The ___glass___ is on the plate.

The pup is in front of the ___plant___.

The kids sit on the ___slide___.

138p

H Look and Write.

glass	glove	glue	glider
glass	glove	glue	glider

slide	sled	slice	slim
slide	sled	slice	slim

plane	plate	plan	plant
plane	plate	plan	plant

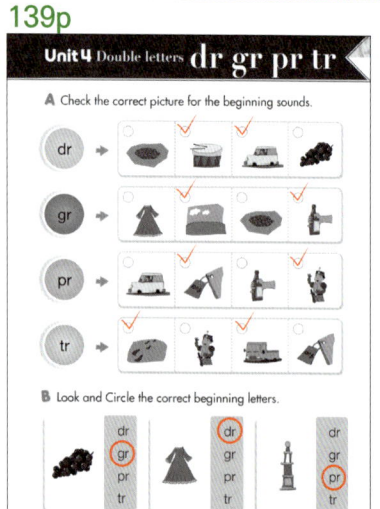
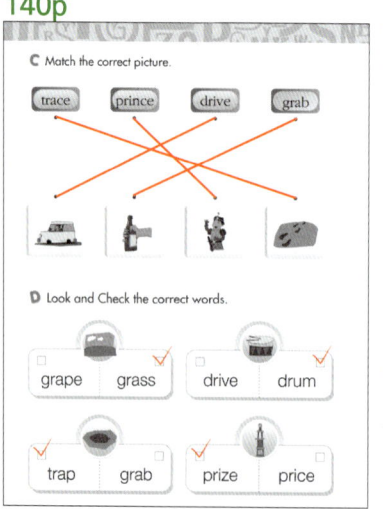
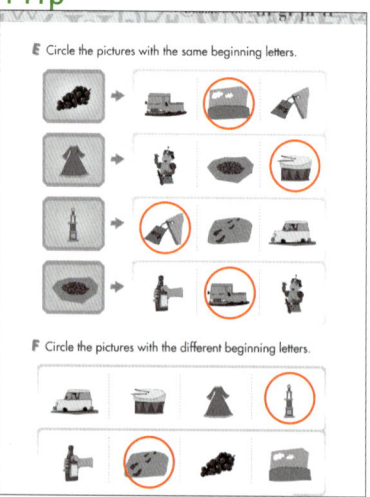

139p

Unit 4 Double letters dr gr pr tr

A Check the correct picture for the beginning sounds.

dr →
gr →
pr →
tr →

B Look and Circle the correct beginning letters.

dr	dr	dr
gr	gr	gr
pr	pr	pr
tr	tr	tr

140p

C Match the correct picture.

trace prince drive grab

D Look and Check the correct words.

| grape | grass | drive | drum |
| trap | grab | prize | price |

141p

E Circle the pictures with the same beginning letters.

F Circle the pictures with the different beginning letters.

Answer Key

142p

G Read and Write the blank.

The kids get the __prize__.

There is a __truck__ in front of the pine.

The bride has __grass__ in the pot.

The prince plays the __drum__.

The crab __trace__ s the slices of ham.

Dad __grab__ s the glass.

143p

H Look and Write.

| dress | drive | drum | grab |
| dress | drive | drum | grab |

| grass | grape | price | prince |
| grass | grape | price | prince |

| prize | truck | trace | trap |
| prize | truck | trace | trap |

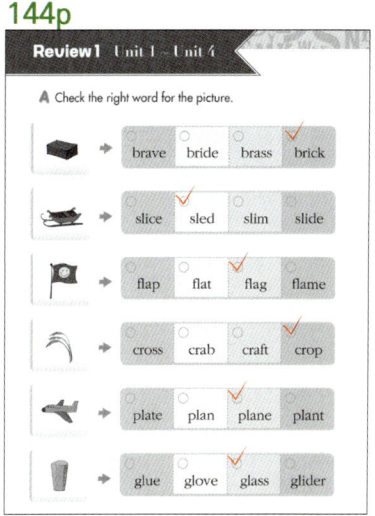

144p

Review 1 Unit 1 - Unit 4

A Check the right word for the picture.

brave | bride | brass | ✓brick

slice | ✓sled | slim | slide

flap | flat | ✓flag | flame

cross | crab | craft | ✓crop

plate | plan | ✓plane | plant

glue | glove | ✓glass | glider

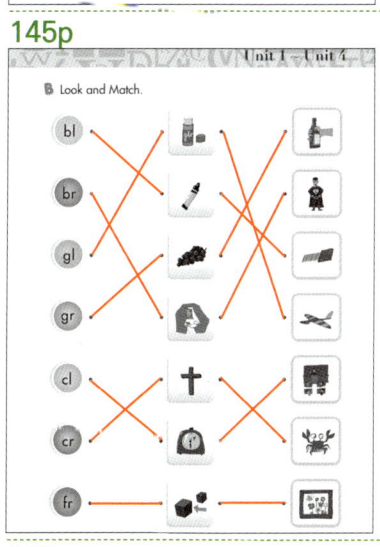

145p

Unit 1 - Unit 4

B Look and Match.

bl
br
gl
gr
cl
cr
fr

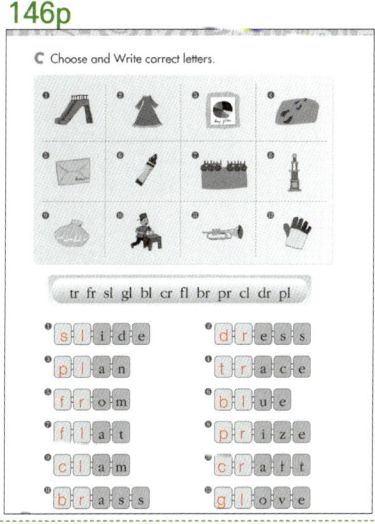

146p

C Choose and Write correct letters.

tr fr sl gl bl cr fl br pr cl dr pl

s l i d e
p l a n
f r o m
f l a t
c l a m
b r a s s

d r e s s
t r a c e
b l u e
p r i z e
c r a f t
g l o v e

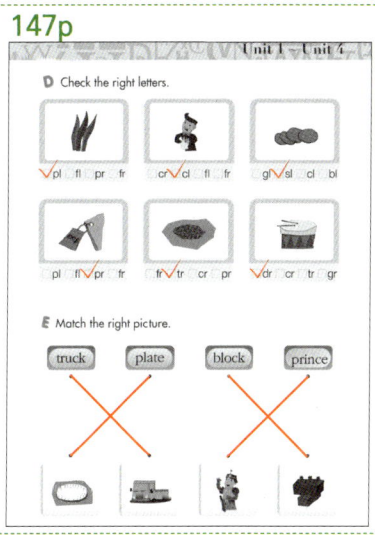

147p

Unit 1 - Unit 4

D Check the right letters.

✓pl fl pr fr | cr ✓cl fl fr | gl ✓sl cl bl

pl ✓fl pr fr | fr ✓tr cr pr | ✓dr cr tr gr

E Match the right picture.

truck | plate | block | prince

148p

F Write the missing letters.

f r og | d r ive | s l im | b l ack

c l ock | f l ag | c r ab | t r ace

g r ape | p l ant | g l ass | b r ave

p r ice | s l ed | g l ove | c l ass

149p

Unit 5 Double letters **sk sm sn st sw**

A Check the correct picture for the beginning sounds.

sk
sw
sn
sm
st

B Look and Circle the correct beginning letters.

sk sm sn st (sw) | (sm) sk sn st sw | sk sm sn (st) sw

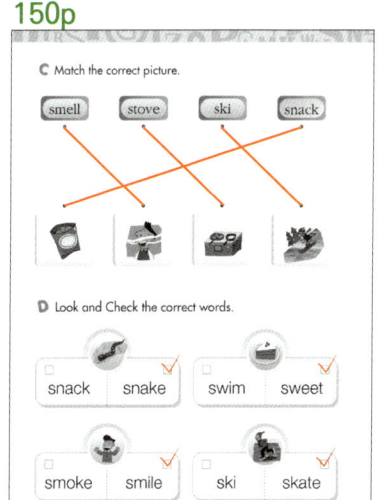

150p

C Match the correct picture.

smell | stove | ski | snack

D Look and Check the correct words.

snack | ✓snake | ✓swim | sweet

smoke | ✓smile | ski | ✓skate

Workbook **181**

151p

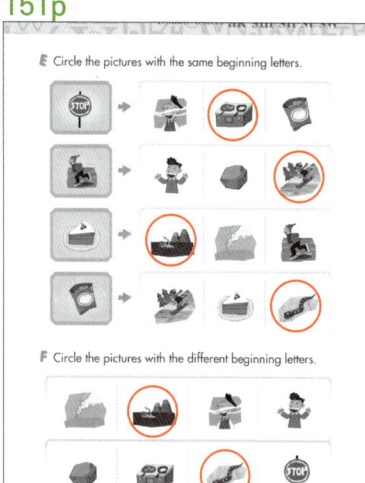

E Circle the pictures with the same beginning letters.

F Circle the pictures with the different beginning letters.

152p

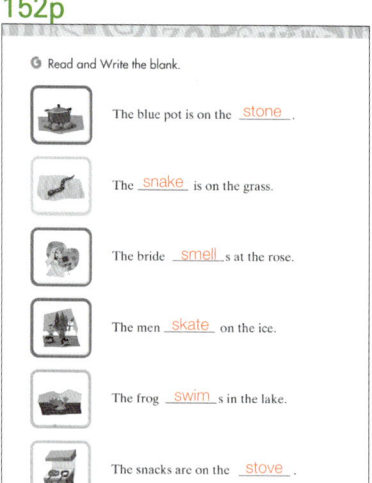

G Read and Write the blank.

The blue pot is on the <u>stone</u>.

The <u>snake</u> is on the grass.

The bride <u>smell</u>s at the rose.

The men <u>skate</u> on the ice.

The frog <u>swim</u>s in the lake.

The snacks are on the <u>stove</u>.

153p

H Look and Write.

ski — ski
skate — skate
swim — swim
sweet — sweet

snack — snack
snake — snake
smile — smile
smoke — smoke

smell — smell
stop — stop
stone — stone
stove — stove

154p

Unit 6 Double letters ng nk ck

A Check the correct picture for the ending sounds.

~ng
~nk
~ck

B Look and Circle the correct ending letters.

155p

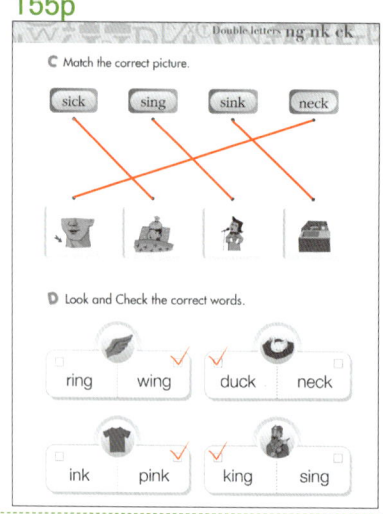

Double letters ng nk ck

C Match the correct picture.

sick   sing   sink   neck

D Look and Check the correct words.

ring   wing   duck   neck
ink   pink   king   sing

156p

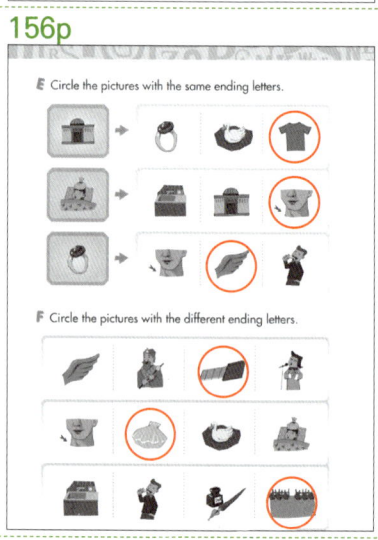

E Circle the pictures with the same ending letters.

F Circle the pictures with the different ending letters.

157p

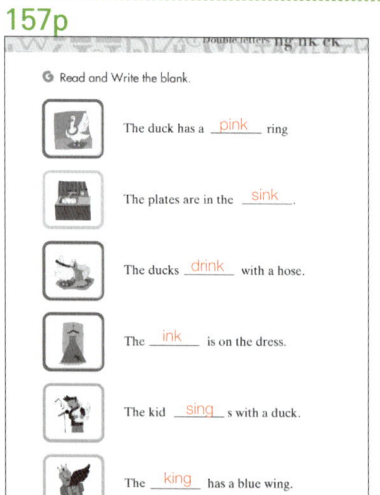

G Read and Write the blank.

The duck has a <u>pink</u> ring

The plates are in the <u>sink</u>.

The ducks <u>drink</u> with a hose.

The <u>ink</u> is on the dress.

The kid <u>sing</u>s with a duck.

The <u>king</u> has a blue wing.

158p

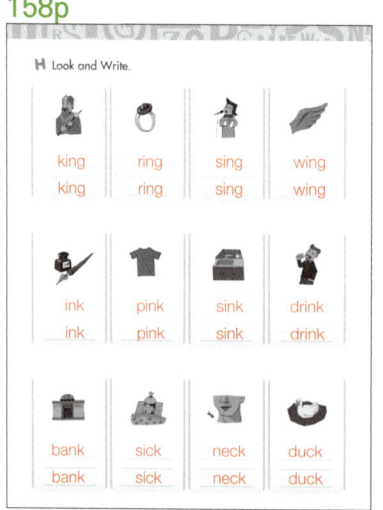

H Look and Write.

king — king
ring — ring
sing — sing
wing — wing

ink — ink
pink — pink
sink — sink
drink — drink

bank — bank
sick — sick
neck — neck
duck — duck

159p

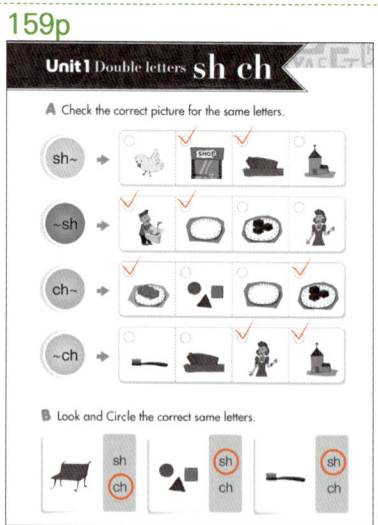

Unit 1 Double letters sh ch

A Check the correct picture for the same letters.

sh~
~sh
ch~
~ch

B Look and Circle the correct same letters.

sh / ch
sh / ch
sh / ch

160p

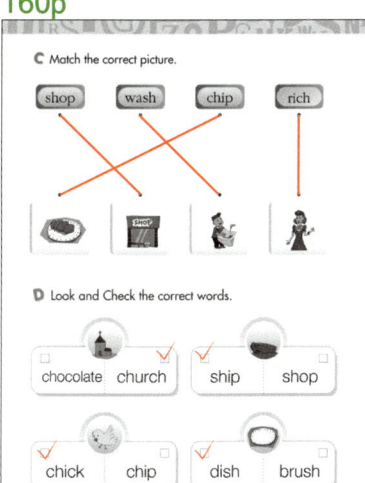

C Match the correct picture.

shop · wash · chip · rich

D Look and Check the correct words.

chocolate · church ✓

ship · shop ✓

chick ✓ · chip

dish ✓ · brush

161p

E Circle the pictures with the same beginning / ending letters.

F Circle the pictures with the different beginning / ending letters.

162p

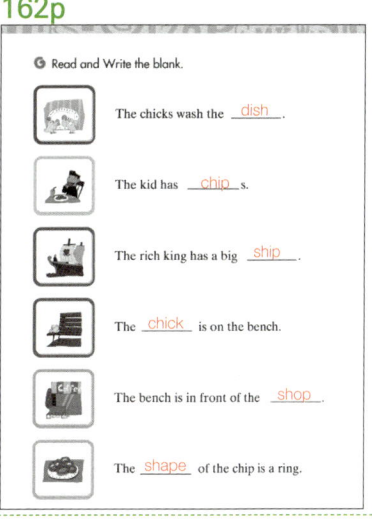

G Read and Write the blank.

The chicks wash the __dish__.

The kid has __chip__ s.

The rich king has a big __ship__.

The __chick__ is on the bench.

The bench is in front of the __shop__.

The __shape__ of the chip is a ring.

163p

H Look and Write.

ship / ship · shop / shop · shape / shape · brush / brush

wash / wash · dish / dish · chick / chick · chip / chip

chocolate / chocolate · bench / bench · rich / rich · church / church

164p

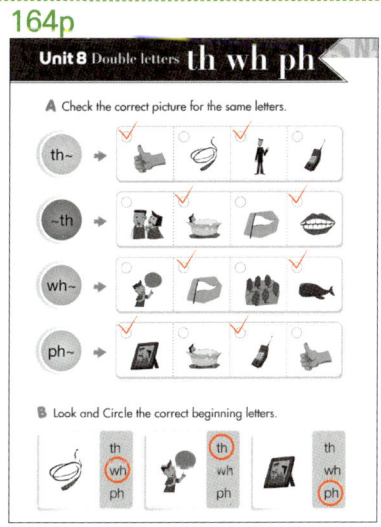

Unit 8 Double letters th wh ph

A Check the correct picture for the same letters.

th~ · ~th · wh~ · ph~

B Look and Circle the correct beginning letters.

th / wh / ph · th / wh / ph · th / wh / ph

165p

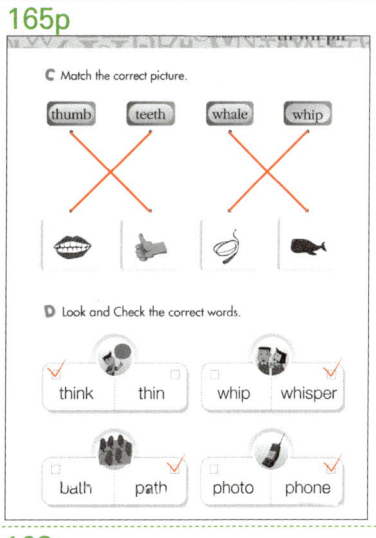

C Match the correct picture.

thumb · teeth · whale · whip

D Look and Check the correct words.

think ✓ · thin

whip · whisper ✓

bath · path ✓

photo ✓ · phone

166p

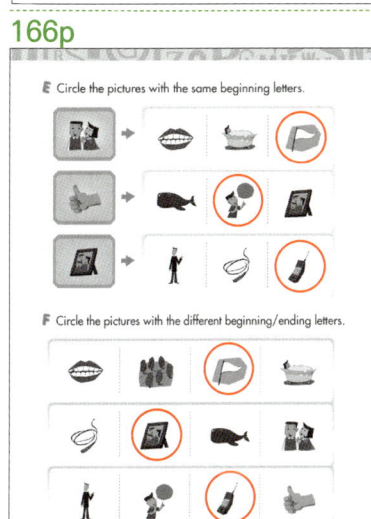

E Circle the pictures with the same beginning letters.

F Circle the pictures with the different beginning / ending letters.

167p

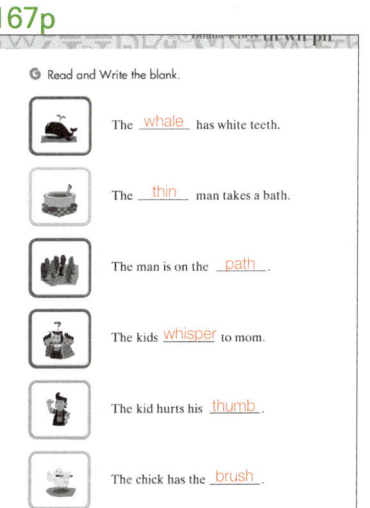

G Read and Write the blank.

The __whale__ has white teeth.

The __thin__ man takes a bath.

The man is on the __path__.

The kids __whisper__ to mom.

The kid hurts his __thumb__.

The chick has the __brush__.

168p

H Look and Write.

thumb / thumb · thin / thin · think / think · bath / bath

path / path · teeth / teeth · whale / whale · white / white

whisper / whisper · whip / whip · photo / photo · phone / phone

Answer Key

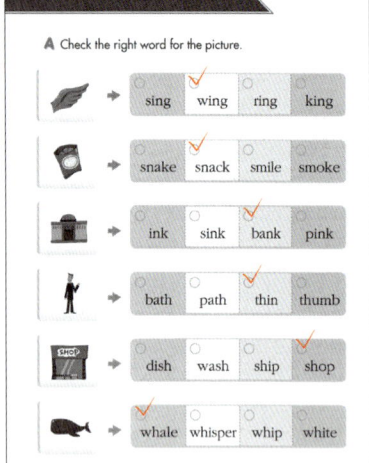

169p
Review 2 Unit 5 ~ Unit 8

A Check the right word for the picture.

- sing / **wing** / ring / king
- snake / **snack** / smile / smoke
- ink / **sink** / bank / pink
- **bath** / path / thin / thumb
- dish / wash / ship / **shop**
- **whale** / whisper / whip / white

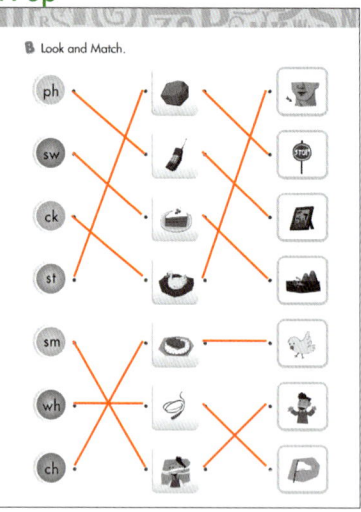

170p
B Look and Match.

- ph
- sw
- ck
- st
- sm
- wh
- ch

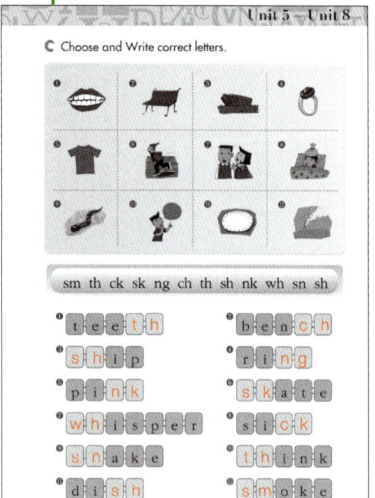

171p
Unit 5 ~ Unit 8

C Choose and Write correct letters.

sm th ck sk ng ch th sh nk wh sn sh

- tee**th**
- **sh**ip
- pi**nk**
- **wh**isper
- **sn**ake
- di**sh**
- be**nch**
- ri**ng**
- **sk**ate
- **s**ick
- **th**ink
- **sm**oke

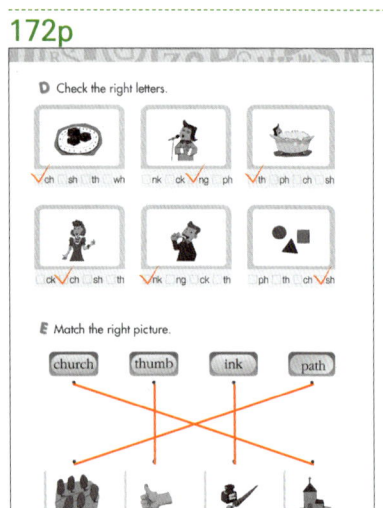

172p
D Check the right letters.

- **ch** / sh / th / wh
- nk / ck / **ng** / ph
- **th** / ph / ch / sh
- ck / **ch** / sh / th
- **nk** / ng / ck / th
- ph / th / ch / **sh**

E Match the right picture.

church thumb ink path

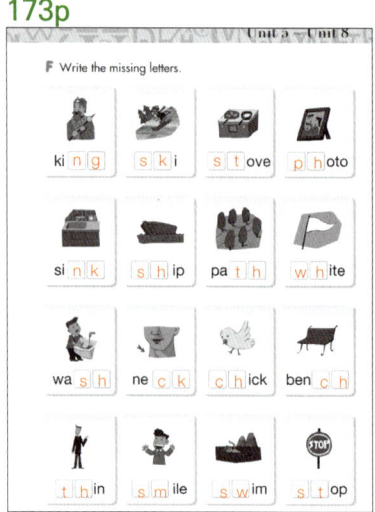

173p
Unit 5 ~ Unit 8

F Write the missing letters.

- ki**ng**
- s**k**i
- **st**ove
- **p**hoto
- si**nk**
- **sh**ip
- pa**th**
- w**h**ite
- wa**sh**
- ne**ck**
- **ch**ick
- ben**ch**
- **th**in
- s**m**ile
- s**w**im
- s**t**op

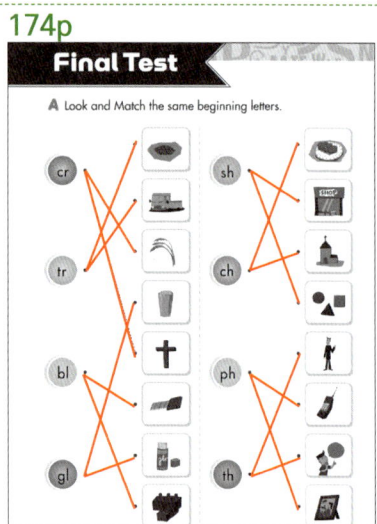

174p
Final Test

A Look and Match the same beginning letters.

- cr
- tr
- bl
- gl
- sh
- ch
- ph
- th

175p
Final Test

B Write the ending letters.

- ri**ng**
- ben**ch**
- tee**th**
- pi**nk**
- di**sh**
- wi**ng**
- du**ck**
- ri**ch**
- dri**nk**
- ne**ck**
- wa**sh**
- ba**th**

176p
C Circle the correct pictures.

- st
- fr
- wh
- sm
- cl
- dr

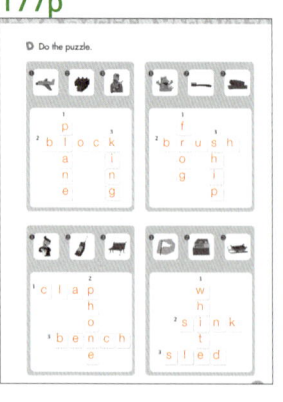

177p
D Do the puzzle.

- p l a n e / b l o c k i n g
- f r o g / b r u s h i p
- c l a p h o n e / b e n c h
- w h i t e / s i n k / s l e d

178p
E Write the correct words.

- chick plant bride bank
- slide ink snake drum
- whip sing grass skate
- smoke prize front blue

184 Workbook